Esoteric Christianity

Cover art by *Jane A Evans*

Esoteric Christianity

The "lesser mysteries"

by **ANNIE BESANT**

*This publication made possible
with the assistance of the Kern Foundation*

THE THEOSOPHICAL PUBLISHING HOUSE

Wheaton, Ill., U.S.A.
Madras, India / London, England

© The Theosophical Publishing House, Adyar

Published 1901. First Quest Abridged Edition 1970
Fourth Quest Printing 1987

A publication of the Theosophical Publishing House,
Wheaton, Illinois, a department of the Theosophical
Society in America.

ISBN 0-8356-0028-9

Printed in the United States of America

IN proceeding to the contemplation of the mysteries of knowledge, we shall adhere to the celebrated and venerable rule of tradition, commencing from the origin of the universe, setting forth those points of physical contemplation which are necessary to be premised, and removing whatever can be an obstacle on the way; so that the ear may be prepared for the reception of the tradition of the Gnosis, the ground being cleared of weeds and fitted for the planting of the vineyard; for there is a conflict before the conflict, and mysteries before the mysteries.—*St. Clement of Alexandria.*

Let the specimen suffice to those who have ears. For it is not required to unfold the mystery, but only to indicate what is sufficient.—*Ibid.*

He that hath ears to hear, let him hear.—*St. Matthew.*

FOREWORD

THE object of this book is to suggest certain lines of thought as to the deep truths underlying Christianity, truths generally overlooked, and only too often denied.

If true knowledge, the Gnosis, is again to form a part of Christian teachings, the study of the Lesser Mysteries must precede that of the Greater. The Greater will never be published through the printing-press; they can only be given by Teacher to pupil, "from mouth to ear." But the Lesser Mysteries, the partial unveiling of deep truths, can even now be restored, and such a volume as the present is intended to outline these, and to show the *nature* of the teachings which have to be mastered. Where only hints are given, quiet meditation on the truths hinted at will cause their outlines to become visible, and the clearer light obtained by continued meditation will gradually show them more fully. For meditation quiets the lower mind, ever engaged in thinking about external objects, and when the lower mind is tranquil, then only can it be illuminated by the Spirit. Knowledge of spiritual truths must be thus obtained, from within and not from without, from the divine Spirit whose temple we are [1] and not from an external Teacher. These things are "spiritually discerned" by that divine

[1] I Cor., iii, 16.

indwelling Spirit, that "mind of Christ," whereof speaks the great Apostle,[1] and that inner light is shed upon the lower mind.

This is the way of the Divine Wisdom, the true THEOSOPHY. It is not, as some think, a diluted version of Hinduism, or Buddhism, or Taoism, or of any special religion. It is Esoteric Christianity as truly as it is Esoteric Buddhism, and belongs equally to all religions, exclusively to none. This is the source of the suggestions made in this little volume, for the helping of those who seek the light—that "true Light which lighteth every man that cometh into the world."[2]

---

[1] I Cor., ii, 14, 16.   [2] St. John, i, 9

CONTENTS

CONTENTS

CHAPTER I

THE HIDDEN SIDE OF RELIGIONS

MANY, perhaps most, who see the title of this book will at once deny that there is anything valuable which can be rightly described as " Esoteric Christianity ". There is a widespread, popular, idea that there is no such thing as an occult teaching in connection with Christianity, and that " The Mysteries ", whether Lesser or Greater, were a purely Pagan institution. The very name of " The Mysteries of Jesus ", so familiar in the ears of the Christians of the first centuries, would come with a shock of surprise on those of their modern successors, and, if spoken as denoting a special and definite institution in the Early Church, would cause a smile of incredulity. It has actually been made a matter of boast that Christianity has no secrets, that whatever it has to say it says to all, and whatever it has to teach it teaches to all. Its truths are supposed to be so simple, that " a wayfaring man, though a fool, may not err therein," and the " simple Gospel " has become a stock phrase.

It is necessary, therefore, to prove clearly that in the Early Church, at least, Christianity was no whit behind other great religions in possessing a hidden side, and that it guarded, as priceless treasures, the secrets revealed only to a select few in its Mysteries. But ere doing this it will be well to consider the whole question of this hidden side of religions, and to see why such a side must exist if a religion is to be strong and stable; for thus its existence in Christianity will appear as a foregone conclusion, and the references to it in the writings of the Christian Fathers will appear simple and natural instead of surprising and unintelligible. As a historical fact, the existence of this esotericism is demonstrable; but it may also be shown that intellectually it is a necessity.

The first question we have to answer is: What is the object of religions? They are given to the world by men wiser than the masses of the people on whom they are bestowed, and are intended to quicken human evolution. In order to do this effectively they must reach individuals and influence them. Now all men are not at the same level of evolution, but evolution might be figured as a rising gradient, with men stationed on it at every point. The most highly evolved are far above the least evolved, both in intelligence and character; the capacity alike to understand and to act varies at every stage. It is, therefore, useless to give to all the same religious teachings. Yet all types need religion, so that each may reach upward to a life higher than that which he is leading, and no type or grade should be sacrificed to any other. Religion must be as graduated as evolution, else it fails in its object.

Next comes the question: In what way do religions seek to quicken human evolution? Religions seek to evolve the moral and intellectual natures, and to aid the spiritual nature to unfold itself. Regarding man as a complex being, they seek to meet him at every point of his constitution, and therefore to bring messages suitable for each, teachings adequate to the most diverse human needs. Teachings must therefore be adapted to each mind and heart to which they are addressed. If a religion does not reach and master the intelligence, if it does not purify and inspire the emotions, it has failed in its object, so far as the person addressed is concerned.

Not only does it thus direct itself to the intelligence and the emotions, but it seeks, as said, to stimulate the unfoldment of the spiritual nature. It answers to that inner impulse which exists in humanity, and which is ever pushing the race onwards. For deeply within the heart of all—often overlaid by transitory conditions, often submerged under pressing interests and anxieties —there exists a continual seeking after God. " As the hart panteth after the water-brooks, so panteth " [1] humanity after God. The search is sometimes checked for a space, and the yearning seems to disappear. Phases recur in civilization and in thought, wherein this cry of the human Spirit for the divine—seeking its source as water seeks its level, to borrow a simile from Giordano Bruno—this yearning of the human Spirit for that which is akin to it in the universe, of the part for the whole, seems to be stilled, to have vanished; none the less does

[1] Psalms, xlii, 1.

that yearning reappear, and once more the same cry rings out from the Spirit. Trampled on for a time, apparently destroyed, though the tendency may be, it rises again and again with inextinguishable persistence, it repeats itseli again and again, no matter how often it is silenced; and it thus proves itself to be an inherent tendency in human nature, an ineradicable constituent thereof. Those who declare triumphantly, " Lo! it is dead! " find it facing them again with undiminished vitality. Those who build without allowing for it find their well-constructed edifices riven as by an earth-quake. Those who hold it to be outgrown find the wildest superstitions succeed its denial. So much is it an integral part of humanity, that man *will* have some answer to his questionings; rather an answer that is false than none. If he cannot find religious truth, he will take religious error rather than no religion, and will accept the crudest and most incongruous ideals rather than admit that the ideal is non-existent.

Religion, then, meets this craving, and taking hold of the constituent in human nature that gives rise to it, trains it, strengthens it, purifies it and guides it towards its proper ending—the union of the human Spirit with the divine, so " that God may be all in all." [1]

The next question which meets us in our inquiry is: What is the source of religions? To this question two answers have been given—that of the comparative mythologists and that of the comparative religionists. Both base their answers on a common basis of

[1] I Cor., xv, 28.

admitted facts. Research has indisputably proved that the religions of the world are markedly similar in their main teachings, in their possession of Founders who display superhuman powers and extraordinary moral elevation, in their ethical precepts, in their use of means to come into touch with invisible worlds, and in the symbols by which they express their leading beliefs. This similarity, amounting in many cases to identity, proves—according to both the above schools —a common origin.

But on the nature of this common origin the two schools are at issue. The comparative mythologists contend that the common origin is the common ignorance, and that the loftiest religious doctrines are simply refined expressions of the guesses of primitive men, regarding themselves and their surroundings. Animism, fetishism, nature-worship, sun-worship—these are the constituents of the primeval mud out of which has grown the splendid lily of religion. A Krishna, a Buddha, a Lao-tze, a Jesus, are the highly civilized but lineal descendants of the whirling medicine-man of the savage. God is a composite photograph of the innumerable Gods who are the personifications of the forces of nature. And so forth. It is all summed up in the phrase: Religions are branches from a common trunk—human ignorance.

The comparative religionists consider, on the other hand, that all religions originate from the teachings of Divine Men, who give out to the different nations of the world, from time to time, such parts of the fundamental verities of religion as the people are capable of receiving, teaching ever the same morality, inculcating the use of similar means, employing the same significant symbols. Sun-worship, and pure forms of nature-worship were, in their day, noble religions, highly allegorical but full of profound truth and knowledge. The great Teachers—it is alleged by Hindus, Buddhists, and by some comparative religionists, such as Theosophists—form an enduring Brotherhood of men who have risen beyond humanity, who appear at certain periods to enlighten the world, and who are the spiritual guardians of the human race. This view may be summed up in the phrase: " Religions are branches from a common trunk —Divine Wisdom."

This Divine Wisdom is spoken of as the Wisdom, the Gnosis, the Theosophia, and some, in different ages of the world, have so desired to emphasize their belief in this unity of religions that they have preferred the eclectic name of Theosophist to any narrower designation.

The relative value of the contentions of these two opposed schools must be judged by the cogency of the evidence put forth by each. The appearance of a degenerate form of a noble idea may closely resemble that of a refined product of a coarse idea, and the only method of deciding between degeneration and evolution would be the examination, if possible, of intermediate and remote ancestors. The evidence brought forward by believers in the Wisdom is of this kind. They allege that the Founders of religions, judged by the records of their teachings, were far above the level of average humanity; that the Scriptures of religions contain moral precepts, sublime ideals, poetical aspirations, profound philosophical statements, which are not even approached in beauty and elevation by later writings in the same religions—that is, that the old is higher than the new, instead of the new being higher than the old; that no case can be shown of the refining and improving process alleged to be the source of current religions, whereas many cases of degeneracy from pure teachings can be adduced; that even among primitive peoples, if their religions be carefully studied, many traces of lofty ideas can be found, ideas which are obviously above the productive capacity of the individuals themselves.

This last idea has been worked out by Mr. Andrew Lang, who—judging by his book on *The Making of Religion*—should be classed as a comparative religionist rather than as a comparative mythologist. He points to the existence of a common tradition and shows, under crude beliefs and degraded views, lofty traditions of a sublime character, touching the nature of the Divine Being and His relations with men. The deities who are worshipped are, for the most part, the veriest devils, but behind, beyond all these, there is a dim but glorious over-arching Presence, seldom or never named, but whispered of as source of all, as power and love and goodness, too tender to awaken terror, too good to require supplication. Such ideas remain as eloquent witnesses of the revelations made by some great Teacher

—dim tradition of whom is generally also discoverable —who was a Son of the Wisdom, and imparted some of its teachings in a long byegone age.

The reason, and, indeed, the justification, of the view taken by the comparative mythologists is patent. They found in every direction low forms of religious belief. These were seen to accompany general lack of civilization. Regarding civilized men as evolving from uncivilized, what more natural than to regard civilized religion as evolving from uncivilized? It is the first obvious idea. Only later and deeper study can show that man in his infancy was not left to grow up untrained, but was nursed and educated by his elders, from whom he received his first guidance alike in religion and civilization. This view is being substantiated by such facts as those dwelt on by Lang, and will presently raise the question, " Who were these elders, of whom traditions are everywhere found? "

Still pursuing our inquiry, we come next to the question: To what people were religions given? And here we come at once to the difficulty with which every Founder of a religion must deal, that already spoken of as bearing on the primary object of religion itself, the quickening of human evolution, with its corollary that all grades of evolving humanity must be considered by Him. Men are at every stage of evolution; in one place there is a highly developed and complex civilization, in another a simple state. Even within any given civilization we find the most varied types— the most ignorant and the most educated, the most thoughtful and the most careless, the most spiritual and the most brutal; yet each of these types must be reached, and each must be helped in the place where he is. If evolution be true, this difficulty is inevitable, and must be faced and overcome by the divine Teacher, else will His work be a failure. If man is evolving as all around him is evolving, these differences of development, these varied grades of intelligence, must be a characteristic of humanity everywhere, and must be provided for in each of the religions of the world.

We are thus brought face to face with the position that we cannot have one and the same religious teaching even for a single nation, still less for a single civilization, or for the whole world. If there be but one teaching, a large number of those to whom it is addressed will entirely escape its influence. If it be made suitable for those whose intelligence is limited, whose morality is elementary, whose perceptions are obtuse, so that it may help and train them, and thus enable them to evolve, it will be a religion utterly unsuitable for those men, living in the same nation, forming part of the same civilization, who have keen and delicate moral perceptions, bright and subtle intelligence, and evolving spirituality. But if, on the other hand, this latter class is to be helped, if intelligence is to be given a philosophy that it can regard as admirable, if delicate moral perceptions are to be still further refined, if the dawning spiritual nature is to be enabled to develop into the perfect day, then the religion will be so spiritual, so intellectual, and so moral, that when it is preached to the former class it will not touch their minds or their hearts, it will be to them a string of meaningless phrases, incapable of arousing their latent intelligence, or of giving them any motive for conduct which will help them to grow into a purer morality.

Looking, then, at these facts concerning religion, considering its object, its means, its origin, the nature and varying needs of the people to whom it is addressed, recognizing the evolution of spiritual, intellectual and moral faculties in man, and the need of each man for such training as is suitable for the stages of evolution at which he has arrived, we are led to the absolute necessity of a varied and graduated religious teaching, such as will meet these different needs and help each man in his own place.

There is yet another reason why esoteric teaching is desirable with respect to a certain class of truths. It is eminently the fact in regard to this class that "knowledge is power". The public promulgation of a philosophy profoundly intellectual, sufficient to train an already highly developed intellect, and to draw the allegiance of a lofty mind, cannot injure any. It can be preached without hesitation, for it does not attract the ignorant, who turn away from it as dry, stiff and uninteresting. But there are teachings which deal with the constitution of nature, explain recondite laws, and throw light on hidden processes, the knowledge of which gives control over natural energies, and enables its possessor to direct these energies to certain ends, as a chemist deals with the production of chemical compounds. Such knowledge may be very useful to highly developed men, and may much increase their power of serving the race. But if this knowledge were published to the world, it might and would be misused, just as the knowledge of subtle poisons was misused in the Middle Ages. It would pass into the hands of people of strong intellect, but of unregulated desires, men moved by separative instincts, seeking the gain of their separate selves and careless of the common good. They would be attracted by the idea of gaining powers which would raise them above the general level, and place ordinary humanity at their mercy, and would rush to acquire the knowledge which exalts its possessors to a superhuman rank. They would, by its possession, become yet more selfish and confirmed in their separateness, their pride would be nourished and their sense of aloofness intensified, and thus they would inevitably be driven along the road which leads to diabolism, the Left Hand Path whose goal is isolation and not union. And they would not only themselves suffer in their inner nature, but they would also become a menace to society, already suffering sufficiently at the hands of men whose intellect is more evolved than their conscience. Hence arises the necessity of withholding certain teachings from those who, morally, are as yet unfitted to receive them; and this necessity presses on every Teacher who is able to impart such knowledge. He desires to give it to those who will use the powers it confers for the general good, for quickening human evolution; but he equally desires to be no party to giving it to those who would use it for their own aggrandisement at the cost of others.

Nor is this a matter of theory only, according to the Occult Records, which give the details of the events alluded to in Genesis vi, *et seq.* This knowledge was, in those ancient times and on the continent of Atlantis, given without any rigid conditions as to the moral elevation, purity and unselfishness of the candidates. Those who were intellectually qualified were taught, just as men are taught ordinary science in modern days. The publicity now so imperiously demanded was then given, with the result that men became giants in knowledge but also giants in evil, till the earth groaned under her oppressors and the cry of a trampled humanity rang through the worlds. Then came the destruction of Atlantis, the whelming of that vast continent beneath the waters of the ocean, some particulars of which are given in the Hebrew Scriptures in the story of the Noachian deluge, and in the Hindu Scriptures of the further East in the story of Vaivasvata Manu.

Since that experience of the danger of allowing unpurified hands to grasp the knowledge which is power, the great Teachers have imposed rigid conditions as regards purity, unselfishness and self-control on all candidates for such instruction. They distinctly refuse to impart knowledge of this kind to any who will not consent to a rigid discipline, intended to eliminate separateness of feeling and interest. They measure the moral strength of the candidate even more than his intellectual development, for the teaching itself will develop the intellect while it puts a strain on the moral nature. Far better that the Great Ones should be assailed by the ignorant for Their supposed selfishness in withholding knowledge, than that They should precipitate the world into another Atlantean catastrophe.

So much of theory we lay down as bearing on the necessity of a hidden side in all religions. When from theory we turn to facts, we naturally ask: Has this hidden side existed in the past, forming a part of the religions of the world? The answer must be an immediate and unhesitating affirmative; every great religion has claimed to possess a hidden teaching, and has declared that it is the repository of theoretical mystic, and further of practical mystic, or occult, knowledge. The mystic explanation of popular teaching was public, and expounded the latter as an allegory, giving to crude and irrational statements and stories a meaning which the intellect could accept. Behind this theoretical mysticism, as it was behind the popular, there existed further the practical mysticism, a hidden spiritual teaching, which was only imparted under definite conditions, conditions known and published, that must be fulfilled by every candidate. St. Clement of Alexandria mentions this division of the Mysteries. After purification, he says, " are the Minor Mysteries, which have some foundation of instruction and of preliminary preparation for what is to come after, and the Great Mysteries, in which nothing remains to be learned of the universe, but only to contemplate and comprehend nature and things." [1]

This position cannot be controverted as regards the ancient religions. The Mysteries of Egypt were the glory of that ancient land, and the noblest sons of Greece, such as Plato, went to Sais and to Thebes to be initiated by Egyptian Teachers of Wisdom. The Mithraic Mysteries of the Persians, the Orphic and Bacchic Mysteries and later Eleusinian semi-Mysteries of the Greeks, the Mysteries of Samothrace, Scythia, Chaldea are familiar in name, at least. Even in the extremely diluted form of the Eleusinian Mysteries, their value is most highly praised by the most eminent men of Greece, as Pindar, Sophocles, Isocrates, Plutarch and Plato. Especially were they regarded as useful with regard to *post mortem* existence, as the Initiated learned that which ensured his future happiness. Sopater further alleged that Initiation established a kinship of the soul with the divine Nature, and in the exoteric Hymn to Demeter covert references are made to the holy child, Iacchus, and to his death and resurrection, as dealt with in the Mysteries. [2]

From Iamblichus, the great theurgist of the third and fourth centuries A.D., much may be learned as to the object of the Mysteries. Theurgy was magic, " the last part of the sacredotal science ", [3] and was practised in

[1] Ante-Nicene Library, Vol. XII, Clement of Alexandria, *Stromata*, bk. V, ch. xl.

[2] See Article on " Mysteries, " *Encyc. Britannica*, ninth edition.

[3] Psellus, quoted in *Iamblichus on the Mysteries*, T. Taylor, p. 343, note on p. 23, second edition.

the Greater Mysteries, to evoke the appearance of superior Beings. The theory on which these Mysteries were based may be very briefly thus stated: There is ONE, prior to all beings, immovable, abiding in the solitude of His own unity. From THAT arises the Supreme God, the Self-begotten, the Good, the Source of all things, the Root, the God of Gods, the First Cause, unfolding Himself into Light.[1] From Him springs the Intelligible World, or ideal universe, the Universal Mind, the *Nous*, and the incorporeal or intelligible Gods belong to this. From this the World-Soul, to which belong the " divine intellectual forms which are present with the visible bodies of the Gods." [2] Then come various hierarchies of superhuman beings, Archangels, Archons (Rulers) or Cosmocratores, Angels, Daimons, etc. Man is a being of a lower order, allied to these in his nature, and is capable of knowing them; this knowledge was achieved in the Mysteries, and it led to union with God.[3] In the Mysteries these doctrines are expounded, " the progression from, and the regression of all things to, the One,

---

[1] *Iamblichus*, as *ante*, p. 301.

[2] *Ibid.*, p. 72.

[3] The article on "Mysticism" in the *Encyclopaedia Britannica* has the following on the teaching of Plotinus (204—206 A.D.): "The One (the Supreme God spoken of above) is exalted above the *nous* and the ' ideas'; it transcends existence altogether and is not cognizable by reason. Remaining itself in repose, it rays out, as it were, from its own fulness, an image of itself, which is called *nous*, and which constitutes the system of ideas of the intelligible world. The soul is in turn the image or product of the *nous*, and the soul by its motion begets corporeal matter. The soul thus faces two ways—towards the *nous* from which it springs, and towards the material life, which is its own product. Ethical endeavour consists in the repudiation of the sensible; material

and the entire domination of the One," [1] and, further, these different Beings were evoked, and appeared, sometimes to teach, sometimes, by Their mere presence, to elevate and purify. "The Gods," says Iamblichus, "being benevolent and propitious, impart their light to theurgists in unenvying abundance, calling upwards their souls to themselves, procuring them a union with themselves, and accustoming them, while they are yet in body, to be separated from bodies, and to be led round to their eternal and intelligible principle." [2] For "the soul having a twofold life, one being in conjunction with body, but the other being separate from all body," [3] it is most necessary to learn to separate it from the body, that thus it may unite itself with the Gods by its intellectual and divine part, and learn the geniune principles of knowledge, and the truths of the intelligible world.[4] "The presence of the Gods, indeed, imparts to us health of body, virtue of soul, purity of intellect, and, in one word, elevates everything in us to its proper

existence is itself estrangement from God. . . . To reach the ultimate goal, thought itself must be left behind; for thought is a form of motion, and the desire of the soul is for the motionless rest which belongs to the One. The union with transcendent deity is not so much knowledge or vision as ecstasy, coalescence, *contact*." Neo-Platonism is thus "first of all a system of complete rationalism; it is assumed, in other words, that reason is capable of mapping out the whole system of things. But, inasmuch as a God is affirmed beyond reason, the mysticism becomes in a sense the necessary complement of the would-be all-embracing rationalism. The system culminates in a mystical act."

[1] *Iamblichus*, as *ante*, p. 73.

[2] *Ibid.*, pp. 55, 56.

[3] *Ibid.*, pp. 118, 119.

[4] *Ibid.*, pp. 118, 119.

nature. It exhibits that which is not body as body to the eyes of the soul, through those of the body." [1] When the Gods appear, the soul receives " a liberation from the passions, a transcendent perfection, and an energy entirely more excellent, and participates of divine love and an immense joy." [2] By this we gain a divine life, and are rendered in reality divine.[3]

The culminating point of the Mysteries was when the Initiate became a God, whether by union with a divine Being outside himself, or by the realization of the divine Self within him. This was termed ecstasy, and was a state of what the Indian Yogi would term high Samadhi, the gross body being entranced and the freed soul effecting its own union with the Great One. This " ecstasy is not a faculty properly so called, it is a state of the soul, which transforms it in such a way that it then perceives what was previously hidden from it. The state will not be permanent until our union with God is irrevocable; here, in earth life, ecstasy is but a flash. . . . Man can cease to become man, and become God; but man cannot be God and man at the same time." [4] Plotinus states that he had reached this state " but three times as yet ".

So also Proclus taught that the one salvation of the soul was to return to her intellectual form, and thus escape from the " circle of generation, from abundant

[1] *Iamblichus*, pp. 95, 100.
[2] *Ibid.*, p. 101.
[3] *Ibid.*, p. 330.
[4] G. R. S. Mead, *Plotinus*, p. 42.

wanderings," and reach true Being, " to the uniform and simple energy of the period of sameness, instead of the abundantly wandering motion of the period which is characterized by difference." This is the life sought by those initiated by Orpheus into the Mysteries of Bacchus and Proserpine, and this the result of the practice of the purificatory, or cathartic, virtues.[1]

These virtues were necessary for the Greater Mysteries, as they concerned the purifying of the subtle body, in which the soul worked when out of the gross body. The political or practical virtues belonged to man's ordinary life, and were required to some extent before he could be a candidate even for such a School as is described below. Then came the cathartic virtues, by which the subtle body, that of the emotions and lower mind, was purified; third the intellectual, belonging to the Augöeides, or the light-form of the intellect; fourth the contemplative, or paradigmatic, by which union with God was realized. Porphyry writes: " He who energizes according to the practical virtues is a worthy man; but he who energizes according to the purifying virtues is an angelic man, or is also a good daimon. He who energizes according to the intellectual virtues alone is a God; but he who energizes according to the paradigmatic virtues is the Father of the Gods." [2]

Much instruction was also given in the Mysteries by the archangelic and other hierarchies, and Pythagoras, the great teacher who was initiated in India, and who

[1] *Iamblichus*, p. 364, note on p. 134.
[2] G. R. S. Mead, *Orpheus*, pp. 285, 286.

gave " the knowledge of things that are " to his pledged disciples, is said to have possessed such a knowledge of music that he could use it for the controlling of men's wildest passions, and the illuminating of their minds. Of this, instances are given by Iamblichus in his *Life of Pythagoras*. It seems probable that the title of Theodidaktos, given to Ammonius Saccas, the master of Plotinus, referred less to the sublimity of his teachings than to this divine instruction received by him in the Mysteries.

Some of the symbols used are explained by Iamblichus,[1] who bids Porphyry remove from his thought the image of the thing symbolized and reach its intellectual meaning. Thus " mire " meant everything that was bodily and material; the " God sitting above the lotus" signified that God transcended both the mire and the intellect, symbolized by the lotus, and was established in Himself, being seated. If " sailing in a ship," His rule over the world was pictured. And so on.[2] On this use of symbols Proclus remarks that "the Orphic method aimed at revealing divine things by means of symbols, a method common to all writers of divine lore." [3]

The Pythagorean School in Magna Graecia was closed at the end of the sixth century B.C., owing to the persecution of the civil power, but other communities existed, keeping up the sacred tradition.[4]   Mead

---

[1] *Iamblichus*, p. 364, note on p. 134.

[2] *Ibid.*, p. 285, *et seq.*

[3] G. R. S. Mead, *Orpheus*, p. 59.

[4] *Ibid.*

states that Plato intellectualized it, in order to protect it from an increasing profanation, and the Eleusinian rites preserved some of its forms, having lost its substance. The Neo-Platonists inherited from Pythagoras and Plato, and their works should be studied by those who would realize something of the grandeur and the beauty preserved for the world in the Mysteries.

The Pythagorean School itself may serve as a type of the discipline enforced. On this Mead gives many interesting details,[1] and remarks: " The authors of antiquity are agreed that this discipline had succeeded in producing the highest examples, not only of the purest chastity and sentiment, but also a simplicity of manners, a delicacy, and a taste for serious pursuits which was unparalleled. This is admitted even by Christian writers." The School had outer disciples, leading the family and social life, and the above quotation refers to these. In the inner School were three degrees—the first of Hearers, who studied for two years in silence, doing their best to master the teachings; the second degree was of Mathematici, wherein were taught geometry and music, the nature of number, form, colour and sound; the third degree was of Physici, who mastered cosmogony and metaphysics. This led up to the true Mysteries. Candidates for the School must be " of an unblemished reputation and of a contented disposition."

The close identity between the methods and aims pursued in these various Mysteries and those of Yoga in India is patent to the most superficial observer. It

[1] G. R. S. Mead, *Orpheus*, pp. 263, 271.

is not, however, necessary to suppose that the nations of antiquity drew from India; all alike drew from the one source, the Grand Lodge of Central Asia, which sent out its Initiates to every land. They all taught the same doctrines, and pursued the same methods, leading to the same ends. But there was much intercommunication between the Initiates of all nations, and there was a common language and a common symbolism. Thus Pythagoras journeyed among the Indians, and received in India a high Initiation, and Apollonius of Tyana later followed in his steps. Quite Indian in phrase as well as thought were the dying words of Plotinus: "Now I seek to lead back the Self within me to the All-self." [1]

Among the Hindus the duty of teaching the supreme knowledge only to the worthy was strictly insisted on. "The deepest mystery of the end of knowledge . . . is not to be declared to one who is not a son or a pupil, and who is not tranquil in mind." [2] So again, after a sketch of Yoga we read: "Stand up! awake! having found the Great Ones, listen! The road is as difficult to tread as the sharp edge of a razor. Thus say the wise." [3] The Teacher is needed, for written teaching alone does not suffice. The "end of knowledge" is to know God —not only to believe; to become one with God—not only to worship afar off. Man must know the reality of the divine Existence, and then know—not only vaguely

[1] G. R. S. Mead, *Plotinus.*
[2] *Shvetashvataropanishat*, vi, 22.
[3] *Kathopanishat*, iii, 14.

believe and hope—that his own innermost Self is one with God, and that the aim of life is to realize that unity. Unless religion can guide a man to that realization, it is but " as sounding brass or a tinkling cymbal." [1]

So also it was asserted that man should learn to leave the gross body: " Let a man with firmness separate it (the soul) from his own body, as a grass-stalk from its sheath." [2]   And it was written: " In the golden highest sheath dwells the stainless, changeless Brahman; It is the radiant white Light of lights, known to the knowers of the Self." [3]   " When the seer sees the golden-coloured Creator, the Lord, the Spirit, whose womb is Brahman, then having thrown away merit and demerit, stainless, the wise one reaches the highest union." [4]

Nor were the Hebrews without their secret knowledge and their Schools of Initiation.   The company of prophets at Naioth presided over by Samuel [5] formed such a School, and the oral teaching was handed down by them.   Similar Schools existed at Bethel and Jericho, [6] and in Cruden's *Concordance* [7] there is the following interesting note: " The Schools or Colleges of the prophets are the first (schools) of which we have any account in Scripture; where the children of the prophets,

---

[1] I. Cor., xiii, 1.
[2] *Kathopanishat*, vi, 17.
[3] *Mundakopanishat*, II, ii, 9.
[4] *Ibid.*, III, i, 3.
[5] I Sam., xix, 20.
[6] II Kings, ii, 2, 5.
[7] Under " School."

that is, their disciples, lived in the exercises of a retired and austere life, in study and meditation, and reading of the law of God. . . . These Schools, or Societies, of the prophets were succeeded by the Synagogues." The *Kabbala*, which contains the semi-public teaching, is, as it now stands, a modern compilation, part of it being the work of Rabbi Moses de Leon, who died A.D. 1305. It consists of five books, Bahir, Zohar, Sepher Sephiroth, Sepher Yetzirah, and Asch Metzareth, and is asserted to have been transmitted orally from very ancient times—as antiquity is reckoned historically. Dr. Wynn Westcott says that " Hebrew tradition assigns the oldest parts of the Zohar to a date antecedent to the building of the second Temple "; and Rabbi Simeon ben Jochai is said to have written down some of it in the first century A.D.   The Sepher Yetzirah is spoken of by Saadiah Gaon, who died A.D. 940, as " very ancient." [1]   Some portions of the ancient oral teaching have been incorporated in the *Kabbala* as it now stands, but the true archaic wisdom of the Hebrews remains in the guardianship of a few of the true sons of Israel.

Brief as is this outline, it is sufficient to show the existence of a hidden side in the religions of the world outside Christianity, and we may now examine the question whether Christianity was an exception to this universal rule.

---

[1] Dr. Wynn Westcott.   *Sepher Yetzirah*, p. 9.

CHAPTER II

THE HIDDEN SIDE OF CHRISTIANITY

(a) THE TESTIMONY OF THE SCRIPTURES

HAVING seen that the religions of the past claimed with one voice to have a hidden side, to be custodians of " Mysteries ", and that this claim was endorsed by the seeking of initiation by the greatest men, we must now ascertain whether Christianity stands outside this circle of religions, and alone is without a Gnosis, offering to the world only a simple faith and not a profound knowledge. Were it so, it would indeed be a sad and lamentable fact, proving Christianity to be intended for a class only, and not for all types of human beings. But that it is not so, we shall be able to prove beyond the possibility of rational doubt.

And that proof is the thing which Christendom at this time most sorely needs, for the very flower of Christendom is perishing for lack of knowledge. If the esoteric teaching can be re-established and win patient and earnest students, it will not be long before the occult is also restored. Disciples of the Lesser Mysteries will become candidates for the Greater, and with the regaining of knowledge will come again the authority of teaching. And truly the need is great. For, looking at the world around us, we find that religion in the West is suffering from the very difficulty that theoretically we should expect to find. Christianity, having lost its mystic and esoteric teaching, is losing its hold on a large number of the more highly educated, and crowds of thoughtful and moral people have slipped away from the churches, because the teachings they received there outraged their intelligence and shocked their moral sense. It is idle to pretend that the widespread agnosticism of this period had its root either in lack of morality or in deliberate crookedness of mind. Everyone who carefully studied the phenomena presented will admit that men of strong intellect have been driven out of Christianity by the crudity of the religious ideas set before them, the contradictions in the authoritative teachings, the views as to God, man and the universe that no trained intelligence could possibly admit. Nor can it be said that any kind of moral degradation lay at the root of the revolt against the dogmas of the Church. The rebels were not too bad for their religion; on the contrary, it was the religion that was too bad for them. The rebellion against popular Christianity was due to the awakening and the growth of conscience; it was the conscience that revolted, as well as the intelligence, against teachings dishonouring to God and man alike, that represented God as a tyrant, and man as essentially evil, gaining salvation by slavish submission.

The reason for this revolt lies in the gradual descent of Christian teaching into so-called simplicity, so that the most ignorant might be able to grasp it. Protestant religionists asserted loudly that nothing ought to be preached save that which every one could grasp, that the glory of the Gospel lay in its simplicity, and that the child and the unlearned ought to be able to understand and apply it to life. True enough, if by this it were meant that there are some religious truths that all can grasp, and that a religion fails if it leaves the most ignorant outside the pale of its elevating influence. But false, utterly false, if by this it be meant that religion has no truths that the ignorant cannot understand, that it is so poor and limited a thing that it has nothing to teach which is above the thought of the intelligent or above the moral purview of the degraded. False, fatally false, if such be the meaning; for as that view spreads, occupying the pulpits and being sounded in the churches, many noble men and women withdraw from the churches. They pass either into a state of passive agnosticism, or—if they be young and enthusiastic—into a condition of active aggression, not believing that that can be the highest which outrages alike intellect and conscience, and preferring the honesty of open unbelief to the drugging of the intellect and the conscience at the bidding of an authority in which they recognize nothing that is divine.

In thus studying the thought of our time we see that the question of a hidden teaching in connection with Christianity becomes of vital importance. Is Christianity to survive as *the* religion of the West? Is it to live through the centuries of the future, and to continue to play a part in moulding the thought of the evolving western races? If it is to live, it must regain the knowledge it has lost, and again have its mystic and its occult teachings; it must again stand forth as an authoritative teacher of spiritual verities, clothed with the only authority worth anything, the authority of knowledge. If these teachings be regained, their influence will soon be seen in wider and deeper views of truth; dogmas, which now seem like mere shells and fetters, shall again be seen to be partial presentments of fundamental realities. First, Esoteric Christianity will reappear in the " Holy Place ", in the Temple, so that all who are capable of receiving it may follow its lines of published thought; and secondly, Occult Christianity will again descend into the adytum, dwelling behind the veil which guards the " Holy of Holies ", into which only the Initiate may enter. Then again will occult teaching be within the reach of those who qualify themselves to receive it, according to the ancient rules, those who are willing in modern days to meet the ancient demands, made on all those who would fain know the reality and truth of spiritual things.

Once again we turn our eyes to history, to see whether Christianity was unique among religions in having no inner teaching, or whether it resembled all others in possessing this hidden treasure. Such a question is a matter of evidence, not of theory, and must be decided by the authority of the existing documents and not by the mere *ipse dixit* of modern Christians.

As a matter of fact both the " New Testament " and the writings of the early Church make the same declarations as to the possession by the Church of such teachings, and we learn from these the fact of the existence of Mysteries—called the Mysteries of Jesus, or the Mysteries of the Kingdom—the conditions imposed on candidates, something of the general nature of the teachings given, and other details. Certain passages in the " New Testament " would remain entirely obscure, if it were not for the light thrown on them by the definite statements of the Fathers and Bishops of the Church, but in that light they become clear and intelligible.

It would indeed have been strange had it been otherwise when we consider the lines of religious thought which influenced primitive Christianity. Allied to the Hebrews, the Persians, and the Greeks, tinged by the older faiths of India, deeply coloured by Syrian and Egyptian thought, this later branch of the great religious stem could not do other than again re-affirm the ancient traditions, and place in the grasp of western peoples the full treasure of the ancient teaching. " The faith once delivered to the saints " would indeed have been shorn of its chief value if, when delivered to the West, the pearl of esoteric teaching had been withheld.

The first evidence to be examined is that of the " New Testament ". For our purpose we may put aside all the vexed questions of different readings and different authors, that can only be decided by scholars. Critical scholarship has much to say on the age of MSS., on the authenticity of documents, and so on. But we need not concern ourselves with these. We may accept the canonical Scriptures, as showing what was believed in the early Church as to the teaching of the Christ and of His immediate followers, and see what they say as to the existence of a secret teaching given only to the few. Having seen the words put into the mouth of Jesus Himself, and regarded by the Church as of supreme authority, we will look at the writings of the great apostle St. Paul; then we will consider the statements made by those who inherited the apostolic tradition and guided the Church during the first centuries A.D.   Along this unbroken line of tradition and written testimony the proposition that Christianity had a hidden side can be established.   We shall further find that the Lesser Mysteries of mystic interpretation can be traced through the centuries to the beginning of the 19th century, and that though there were no Schools of Mysticism recognized as preparatory to Initiation, after the disappearance of the Mysteries, yet great mystics, from time to time, reached the lower stages of ecstasy, by their own sustained efforts, aided doubtless by invisible Teachers.

The words of the Master Himself are clear and definite, and were, as we shall see, quoted by Origen as referring to the secret teaching preserved in the Church. " And when he was alone, they that were about him with the twelve asked of him the parable. And he said unto them, ' Unto you it is given to know the mystery of the kingdom of God, but unto them that are without, all these things are done in parables.' "   And later: " With many such parables spake he the word unto them, as they were able to hear it. But without a parable spake he not unto them; and when they were alone he expounded all things to his disciples." [1] Mark the significant words, " when they were alone," and the phrase, " them that are without." So also in the version of St. Matthew: " Jesus sent the multitude away, and went into the house; and his disciples came unto him." These teachings given " in the house ", the innermost meanings of his instructions, were alleged to be handed on from teacher to teacher. The Gospel gives, it will be noted, the allegorical mystic explanation, that which we have called The Lesser Mysteries, but the deeper meaning was said to be given only to the Initiates.

Again, Jesus tells even his apostles: " I have yet many things to say to you, but ye cannot bear them now." [2] Some of them were probably said after his death, when he was seen of his disciples, " speaking of the things pertaining to the kingdom of God." [3] None of these have been publicly recorded, but who can believe that they were neglected or forgotten, and were not handed down as a priceless possession? There was a tradition in the Church that he visited his apostles for a considerable period after his death, for the sake of giving them instruction—a fact that will be referred to later—and in the famous Gnostic treatise, the *Pistis Sophia*, we read: " It came to pass, when Jesus had

---

[1] St. Mark, iv, 10, 11, 33, 34. See also St. Matt., xiii, 11, 34, 36, and St. Luke, viii, 10.

[2] St. John, xvi, 12.

[3] Acts, i, 3.

risen from the dead, that he passed eleven years speaking with his disciples and instructing them." [1] Then there is the phrase, which many would fain soften and explain away: " Give not that which is holy to the dogs, neither cast ye your pearls before swine " [2]—a precept which is of general application indeed, but was considered by the early Church to refer to the secret teachings. It should be remembered that the words had not the same harshness of sound in the ancient days as they have now; for the word " dogs "—like " the vulgar ", " the profane "—was applied by those within a certain circle to all who were outside its pale, whether by a society or association, or by a nation—as by the Jews to all Gentiles.[3] It was sometimes used to designate those who were outside the circle of Initiates, and we find it employed in that sense in the early Church; those who, not having been initiated into the Mysteries, were regarded as being outside " the kingdom of God ", or " the spiritual Israel ", had this name applied to them.

There were several names, exclusive of the term " The Mystery", or " The Mysteries ", used to designate the sacred circle of the Initiates or connected with Initiation: " The Kingdom", " The Kingdom of God ", " The Kingdom of Heaven ", " The Narrow Path ", " The Strait Gate", " The Perfect ", " The Saved ", " Life Eternal", " Life", " The Second Birth", " A Little

---

[1] *Loc. cit.*   Trans. by G. R. S. Mead, I, i, 1.

[2] St. Matt., vii, 6.

[3] As to the Greek woman: " It is not meet to take the childrens' bread, and to cast it unto the dogs."—St. Mark, vii, 27.

One ", " A Little Child ". The meaning is made plain
by the use of these words in early Christian writings,
and in some cases even outside the Christian pale. Thus
the term, " The Perfect ", was used by the Essenes, who
had three orders in their communities: the Neophytes,
the Brethren, and the Perfect—the last being Initiates;
and it is employed generally in that sense in old writings.
" The Little Child " was the ordinary name for a candidate just initiated, *i.e.*, who had just taken his " second
birth ".

When we know this use, many obscure and otherwise
harsh passages become intelligible. " Then said one
unto Him: Lord, are there few that be saved? And he
said unto them: Strive to enter in at the strait gate; for
many, I say unto you, will seek to enter in and shall
not be able." [1] If this be applied in the fundamentalist
way to salvation from everlasting hell-fire, the statement becomes incredible, shocking. No Saviour of
the world can be supposed to assert that many will
seek to avoid hell and enter heaven, but will not be able
to do so. But as applied to the narrow gateway of
Initiation and to salvation from rebirth, it is perfectly
true and natural. So again: " Enter ye in at the strait
gate; for wide is the gate and broad is the way that
leadeth to destruction, and many there be which go in
thereat; because strait is the gate and narrow is the way
which leadeth unto life; and few there be that find it." [2]
The warning which immediately follows against the false

[1] St. Luke, xiii, 23, 24.
[2] St. Matt., vii, 13, 14.

prophets, the teachers of the dark Mysteries, is most apposite in this connection. No student can miss the familiar ring of these words used in this same sense in other writings. The " ancient narrow way " is familiar to all: the path " difficult to tread as the sharp edge of a razor," [1] already mentioned; the going " from death to death " of those who follow the flower-strewn path of desires, who do not know God; for those men only become immortal and escape from the wide mouth of death, from ever repeated destruction, who have quitted all desires.[2] The allusion to death is, of course, to the repeated births of the soul into gross material existence, regarded always as " death " compared to the " life " of the higher and subtler worlds.

This " Strait Gate " was the gateway of Initiation, and through it a candidate entered " The Kingdom." And it ever has been, and must be, true that only a few can enter that gateway, though myriads—an exceedingly " great multitude, which no man could number," [3] not a few—enter into the happiness of the heaven-world. So also spoke another great Teacher, nearly three thousand years earlier: " Among thousands of men scarce one striveth for perfection; of the successful strivers scarce one knoweth Me in essence." [4] For the Initiates are few in each generation, the flower of humanity; but no gloomy sentence of everlasting woe is pronounced in

---

[1] *Kathopanishat*, II, iv, 10, 11.

[2] *Brahadaranyakopanishat*, IV, iv, 7.

[3] Rev., xii, 9.

[4] *Bhagavad Gita*, vii, 3.

this statement on the vast majority of the human race. The saved are, as Proclus taught,[1] those who escape from the circle of generation, within which humanity is bound.

In this connection we may recall the story of the young man who came to Jesus, and, addressing him as "Good Master," asked how he might win eternal life—the well-recognized liberation from rebirth by knowledge of God.[2] His first answer was the regular exoteric precept: "Keep the commandments." But when the young man answered: "All these things have I kept from my youth up", then, to that conscience free from all knowledge of transgression, came the answer of the true Teacher: "If thou will be perfect, go and sell that thou hast, and give to the poor, and thou shalt have treasure in heaven; and come and follow me." "If thou wilt be perfect," be a member of the Kingdom, poverty and obedience must be embraced. And then to His own disciples Jesus explains that a rich man can hardly enter the Kingdom of Heaven, such entrance being more difficult than for a camel to pass through the eye of a needle; with men such entrance could not be, with God all things were possible.[3] Only God in man can pass that barrier.

This text has been variously explained away, it being obviously impossible to take it in its surface meaning, that a rich man cannot enter a post-mortem state of

[1] *Ante*, p. 19.

[2] It must be remembered that the Jews believed that all imperfect souls returned to live again on earth.

[3] St. Matt., xiv, 16-26.

happiness. Into that state the rich man may enter as well as the poor, and the universal practice of Christians shows that they do not for one moment believe that riches imperil their happiness after death. But if the real meaning of the Kingdom of Heaven be taken, we have the expression of a simple and direct fact. For that knowledge of God which is Eternal Life [1] cannot be gained till everything earthly is surrendered, cannot be learned until everything has been sacrificed. The man must give up not only earthly wealth, which henceforth may only pass through his hands as steward, but he must give up his inner wealth as well, as far as he holds it as his own against the world; until he is stripped naked he cannot pass the narrow gateway. Such has ever been a condition of Initiation, and " poverty, obedience, chastity," has been the vow of the candidate.

The " second birth " is another well-recognized term for Initiation; even now in India the higher castes are called " twice-born," and the ceremony that makes them twice-born is a ceremony of Initiation—mere husk truly, in these modern days, but the " pattern of things in the heavens." [2] When Jesus is speaking to Nicodemus, He states that " Except a man be born again, he cannot see the kingdom of God," and this birth is spoken of as that " of water and the Spirit " [3] ; this is the first Initiation; a later one is that of " the Holy Ghost and fire," [4]

[1] St. John, xvii, 3.
[2] Heb., ix, 23.
[3] St. John, iii, 3, 5.
[4] St. Matt., iii, 11.

the baptism of the Initiate in his manhood, as the first is that of birth, which welcomes him as " the Little Child " entering the Kingdom.[1] How thoroughly this imagery was familiar among the mystics of the Jews is shown by the surprise evinced by Jesus when Nicodemus stumbled over His mystic phraseology: " Art thou a master of Israel, and knowest not these things ? " [2]

Another precept of Jesus which remains as " a hard saying " to his followers is: " Be ye therefore perfect, even as your Father which is in heaven is perfect." [3] The ordinary Christian knows that he cannot possibly obey this command; full of ordinary human frailties and weaknesses, how can he become perfect as God is perfect? Seeing the impossibility of the achievement set before him, he quietly puts it aside, and thinks no more about it. But seen as the crowning effort of many lives of steady improvement, as the triumph of the God within us over the lower nature, it comes within calculable distance, and we recall the words of Porphyry, how the man who achieves " the paradigmatic virtues is the Father of the Gods," [4] and that in the Mysteries these virtues were acquired.

St. Paul follows in the footsteps of his Master, and speaks in exactly the same sense, but, as might be expected from his organizing work in the Church, with greater explicitness and clearness. The student should

[1] *Ibid.*, xviii, 3.
[2] St. John, iii, 10.
[3] St. Matt., v, 48.
[4] *Ante*, p. 20.

read with attention chapters ii and iii and verse 1 of chapter iv of the First Epistle to the Corinthians, remembering, as he reads, that the words are addressed to baptised and communicant members of the Church, full members from the modern standpoint, although described as babes and carnal by the Apostle. They were not catechumens or neophytes, but men and women who were in complete possession of all the privileges and responsibilities of Church membership, recognized by the Apostle as being separate from the world, and expected not to behave as men of the world. They were in fact, in possession of all that the modern Church gives to its members. Let us summarize the Apostle's words:

" I came to you bearing the divine testimony, not alluring you with human wisdom but with the power of the Spirit. Truly ' we speak wisdom among them that are perfect,' but it is no human wisdom. ' We speak the wisdom of God in a mystery, even the hidden wisdom, which God ordained before the world ' began, and which none even of the princes of this world know. The things of that wisdom are beyond men's thinking, ' but God hath revealed them unto us by his Spirit . . . the deep things of God,' ' which the Holy Ghost teacheth.' [1] These are spiritual things, to be discerned only by the spiritual man, in whom is the mind of Christ.

[1] Note how this chimes in with the promise of Jesus in St. John, xvi, 12-14: " I have yet many things to say unto you, but ye cannot bear them now. Howbeit when He, the Spirit of truth, is come, He will guide you into all truth. . . . He will show you things to come. . . . He shall receive of mine and shall show it unto you."

'And I, brethren, could not speak unto you as unto spiritual, but as unto carnal, even as unto babes in Christ. . . . Ye were not able to bear it, neither yet now are ye able. For ye are yet carnal.' ' As a wise master-builder [1] I have laid the foundation,' and ' ye are the temple of God, and the Spirit of God dwelleth in you.' ' Let a man so account of us, as of the ministers of Christ, and stewards of the Mysteries of God.' "

Can any one read this passage—and all that has been done in the summary is to bring out the salient points —without recognizing the fact that the Apostle possess-ed a divine wisdom given in Mysteries, that his Corin-thian followers were not yet able to receive? And note the recurring technical terms: the " wisdom", the " wis-dom of God in a mystery", the " hidden wisdom", known only to the " spiritual " man, spoken of only among the " perfect", wisdom from which the non-" spiritual", the " babes in Christ", the " carnal", were excluded, known to the " wise master-builder", " the steward of the Mysteries of God."

Again and again he refers to these Mysteries. Writ-ing to the Ephesian Christians he says that " by revela-tion," by the unveiling, had been " made known unto me the Mystery," and hence his " knowledge in the Mystery of Christ "; all might know of the " fellowship of the Mystery." [2] Of this Mystery, he repeated to the Colossians, he was " made a minister ", " the Mystery

[1] Another technical name in the Mysteries.
[2] Eph., iii, 3, 4, 9.

which hath been hid from ages and from generations, but now is made manifest to His saints "; not to the world, nor even to Christians, but only to the Holy Ones. To them was unveiled " the glory of this Mystery "; and what was it? " Christ *in you* "—a significant phrase, which we shall see, in a moment, belonged to the life of the Initiate; thus ultimately must every man learn the wisdom, and become " perfect in Christ Jesus." [1] These Colossians he bids pray " that God would open to us a door of utterance, to speak the mystery of Christ," [2] a passage to which St. Clement refers as one in which the apostle " clearly reveals that knowledge belongs not to all." [3] So also he writes to his loved Timothy, bidding him select his deacons from those who hold " the Mystery of the faith in a pure conscience," that great " Mystery of Godliness " that he had learned,[4] knowledge of which was necessary for the teachers of the Church.

Now St. Timothy holds an important position, as representing the next generation of Christian teachers. He was a pupil of St. Paul, and was appointed by him to guide and rule a portion of the Church. He had been, we learn, initiated into the Mysteries by St. Paul

[1] Col., i, 23, 25-28. But St. Clement, in his *Stromata*, translates " every man ", as " the whole man ". See Bk. V, ch. x.

[2] Col., iv, 3.

[3] Ante-Nicene Library, Vol. XII, Clement of Alexandria, *Stromata*, Bk. V, ch. x. Some additional sayings of the Apostles will be found in the quotations from Clement, showing what meaning they bore in the minds of those who succeeded the Apostles, and were living in the same atmosphere of thought.

[4] I. Tim., iii, 9, 16.

himself, and reference is made to this, the technical phrases once more serving as a clue. " This charge I commit unto thee, son Timothy, according to the prophecies which went before on thee," [1] the solemn benediction of the Initiator, who admitted the candidate; but not alone was the Initiator present: " Neglect not the gift that is in thee, which was given thee by prophecy, by the laying on of the hands of the Presbytery," [2] of the Elder Brothers.   And he reminds him to lay hold of that " eternal life, whereunto thou art also called, and hast professed a good profession before many witnesses " [3]—the vow of the new Initiate, pledged in the presence of the Elder Brothers, and of the assembly of Initiate. The knowledge then given was the sacred charge of which St. Paul cries out so forcibly: " O Timothy, keep that which is committed to thy trust " [4] —not the knowledge commonly possessed by Christians, as to which no special obligation lay upon St. Timothy, but the sacred deposit committed to his trust as an Initiate, and essential to the welfare of the Church. St. Paul later recurs again to this, laying stress on the supreme importance of the matter in a way that would be exaggerated had the knowledge been the common property of Christian men: " Hold fast the form of sound words which thou hast heard of me. . . . That good thing which was committed unto thee, keep by

[1] I. Tim., i, 18.
[2] Ibid., iv, 14.
[3] Ibid., vi, 13.
[4] Ibid., vi, 20.

the Holy Ghost which dwelleth in us " [1]—as serious an adjuration as human lips could frame. Further, it was his duty to provide for the due transmission of this sacred deposit, that it might be handed on to the future, and the Church might never be left without teachers: " The things that thou hast heard of me among many witnesses "—the sacred oral teachings given in the assembly of Initiates, who bore witness to the accuracy of the transmission—" the same commit thou to faithful men, who shall be able to teach others also." [2]

The knowledge—or, if the phrase be preferred, the supposition—that the Church possessed these hidden teachings throws a flood of light on the scattered remarks made by St. Paul about himself, and when they are gathered together, we have an outline of the evolution of the Initiate. St. Paul asserts that though he was already among the Initiated—for he says: " Let us, therefore, as many as be perfect, be thus minded " —he had not yet " attained ", was indeed not yet wholly " perfect ", for he had not yet won Christ, he had not yet reached the " high calling of God in Christ," " the power of his resurrection, and the fellowship of his sufferings, being made conformable unto his death "; and he was striving, he says, " if by any means I might attain unto the resurrection of the dead." [3] For this was the Initiation that liberated, that made the

[1] II. Tim., i, 13, 14.
[2] *Ibid.*, ii, 2.
[3] Phil., iii, 8, 10-12, 14, 15.

Initiate the Perfect Master, the Risen Christ, freeing Him finally from the " dead", from the humanity within the circle of generation, from the bonds that fettered the soul to gross matter. Here again we have a number of technical terms, and even the surface reader should realize that the " resurrection of the dead " here spoken of cannot be the ordinary resurrection of the modern Christian, supposed to be inevitable for all men, and therefore obviously not requiring any special struggle on the part of any one to attain to it. In fact the very word " attain " would be out of place in referring to a universal and inevitable human experience. St. Paul could not avoid *that* resurrection, according to the modern Christian view. What then was the resurrection to attain which he was making such strenuous efforts? Once more the only answer comes from the Mysteries. In them the Initiate approaching the Initiation that liberated from the cycle of rebirth, the circle of generation, was called " the suffering Christ "; he shared the sufferings of the Saviour of the world, was crucified mystically, " made conformable to his death," and then attained the resurrection, the fellowship of the glorified Christ, and after that death had over him no power.[1] This " the prize " towards which the great Apostle was pressing, and he urged " as many as be perfect", *not the ordinary believer*, thus also to strive. Let them not be content with what they had gained, but still press onwards.

[1] Rev., i, 18. " I am He that liveth, and was dead; and behold, I am alive for evermore. Amen."

The resemblance of the Initiate to the Christ is, indeed, the very groundwork of the Greater Mysteries, as we shall see more in detail when we study " The Mystical Christ". The Initiate was no longer to look on Christ as outside himself: " Though we have known Christ after the flesh, yet now henceforth know we Him no more." [1]

The ordinary believer had " put on Christ "; " as many of you as have been baptised into Christ have put on Christ." [2] Then they were the " babes in Christ " to whom reference has already been made, and Christ was the Saviour to whom they looked for help, knowing Him " after the flesh." But when they had conquered the lower nature and were no longer " carnal", then they were to enter on a higher path, and were themselves to become Christ. This which he himself had already reached, was the longing of the Apostle for his followers: " My little children, of whom I travail in birth again until Christ be formed *in you*." [3] Already he was their spiritual father, having " begotten you through the gospel." [4] But now " again " he was as a parent, as their mother to bring them to the second birth. Then the infant Christ, the Holy Christ, was born in the soul, " the hidden man of the heart " [5]; the Initiate thus became that " Little Child "; henceforth he

---

[1] II. Cor., v, 16.

[2] Gal., iii, 27.

[3] Gal., iv, 19.

[4] I. Cor., iv, 15.

[5] I. St. Pet., iii, 4.

was to live out in his own person the life of the Christ, until he became the " perfect man," growing " unto the measure of the stature of the fulness of Christ." [1] Then he, as St. Paul was doing, filled up the sufferings of Christ in his own flesh,[2] and always bore " about in the body the dying of the Lord Jesus," [3] so that he could truly say: " I am crucified with Christ, nevertheless I live; yet not I, but Christ liveth in me." [4] Thus was the Apostle himself suffering; thus he describes himself. And when the struggle is over, how different is the calm tone of triumph from the strained effort of the earlier years: " I am now ready to be offered, and the time of my departure is at hand. I have fought a good fight, I have finished my course, I have kept the faith; henceforth there is laid up for me a crown of righteousness." [5] This was the crown given to " him that overcometh," of whom it is said by the ascended Christ: " I will make him a pillar in the temple of my God; and he shall go no more out." [6] For after the " Resurrection " the Initiate has become the Perfect Man, the Master, and He goes out no more from the Temple, but from it serves and guides the worlds.

It may be well to point out, ere closing this chapter, that St. Paul himself sanctions the use of the theoretical

[1] Eph., iv, 13.
[2] Col., i, 24.
[3] II. Cor., iv, 10.
[4] Gal., ii, 20.
[5] II. Tim., iv, 6, 8.
[6] Rev., iii, 12.

mystic teaching in explaining the historical events recorded in the Scriptures.   The history therein written is
not regarded by him as a mere record of facts, which
occurred on the physical plane.   A true mystic, he saw
in the physical events the shadows of the universal truths
ever unfolding in higher and inner worlds, and knew
that the events selected for preservation in occult writings were such as were typical, the explanation of which
would subserve human instruction.   Thus he takes the
story of Abraham, Sarai, Hagar, Ishmael, and Isaac,
and saying, " which things are an allegory," he proceeds
to give the mystical interpretation.[1]   Referring to the
escape of the Israelites from Egypt, he speaks of the
Red Sea as a baptism, of the manna and the water as
spiritual meat and spiritual drink, of the rock from
which the water flowed as Christ.[2]   He sees the great
mystery of the union of Christ and His Church in the
human relation of husband and wife, and speaks of
Christians as the flesh and the bones of the body of
Christ.[3]   The writer of the Epistle to the Hebrews alle-
gorises the whole Jewish system of worship.   In the
Temple he sees a pattern of the heavenly Temple, in
the High Priest he sees Christ, in the sacrifices the offering of the spotless Son; the priests of the Temple are but
" the example and shadow of heavenly things," of the
heavenly priesthood serving in " the true tabernacle. "
A most elaborate allegory is thus worked out in chapters

[1] Gal., iv, 22-31.
[2] I. Cor., x, 1-4.
[3] Eph,. v, 23-32.

iii-x, and the writer alleges that the Holy Ghost thus signified the deeper meaning; all was " a figure for the time. "

In this view of the sacred writings, it is not alleged that the events recorded did not take place, but only that their physical happening was a matter of minor importance. And such explanation is the unveiling of the Lesser Mysteries, the mystic teaching which is permitted to be given to the world. It is not, as many think, a mere play of the imagination, but is the outcome of a true intuition, seeing the patterns in the heavens, and not only the shadows cast by them on the screen of earthly time.

CHAPTER III

THE HIDDEN SIDE OF CHRISTIANITY

(*Concluded*)

(*b*) THE TESTIMONY OF THE CHURCH

WHILE it may be that some would be willing to admit the possession by the Apostles and their immediate successors of a deeper knowledge of spiritual things than was current among the masses of the believers around them, few will probably be willing to take the next step, and, leaving that charmed circle, accept as the depository of their sacred learning the Mysteries of the Early Church. Yet we have St. Paul providing for the transmission of the unwritten teaching, himself initiating St. Timothy, and instructing St. Timothy to initiate others in his turn, who should again hand it on to yet others. We thus see the provision of four successive generations of teachers, spoken of in the Scriptures themselves, and these could far more than overlap the writers of the Early Church, who bear witness to the existence of the Mysteries. For among these are pupils of the Apostles themselves, though the most definite statements belong to those removed from the Apostles by one intermediate teacher. Now, as soon as we begin to study the writings of the Early Church, we are met by the facts that there are allusions which are only intelligible by the existence of the Mysteries, and then statements that the Mysteries are existing. This might, of course, have been expected, seeing the point at which the New Testament leaves the matter, but it is satisfactory to find the facts answer to the expectation.

The first witnesses are those called the Apostolic Fathers, the disciples of the Apostles; but very little of their writings, and that disputed, remains. Not being written controversially, the statements are not as categorical as those of the later writers. Their letters are for the encouragement of the believers. Polycarp, Bishop of Smyrna, and fellow-disciple with Ignatius of St. John,[1] expresses as hope that his correspondents are " well versed in the sacred Scriptures and that nothing is hid from you; but to me this privilege is not yet granted " [2]—writing, apparently, before reaching full Initiation. Barnabas speaks of communicating " some portion of what I have myself received," [3] and after expounding the Law mystically, declares that " we then, rightly understanding His commandments, explain them

[1] Vol. I. *The Martyrdom of Ignatius*, ch. iii.

The translations used are those of Clarke's Ante-Nicene Library, a most useful compendium of Christian antiquity. The number of the volume which stands first in the references is the number of the volume in that Series.

[2] *Ibid.*, *The Epistle of Polycarp*, ch. xii.

[3] *Ibid.*, *The Epistle of Barnabas*, ch. i.

as the Lord intended." [1]   Ignatius, Bishop of Antioch,
a disciple of St. John.[2] speaks of himself as " not yet
perfect in Jesus Christ.   For I now begin to be a disciple, and I speak to you as my fellow-disciples," [3] and
he speaks of them as " initiated into the mysteries of
the Gospel with Paul, the holy, the martyred." [4]   Again
he says: " Might I not write to you things more full of
mystery? But I fear to do so, lest I should inflict injury
on you who are but babes.   Pardon me in this respect,
lest, as not being able to receive their weighty import,
ye should be strangled by them.   For even I, though I am
bound (for Christ) and am able to understand heavenly things, the angelic orders, and the different sorts
of angels and hosts, the distinction between powers and
dominions, and the diversities between thrones and
authorities, the mightiness of the aeons, and the pre-
eminence of the cherubim and seraphim, the sublimity
of the Spirit, the kingdom of the Lord, and above all
the incomparable majesty of Almighty God—though I
am acquainted with these things, yet am I not therefore
by any means perfect, nor am I such a disciple as Paul
or Peter." [5]   This passage is interesting, as indicating
that the organization of the celestial hierarchies was one
of the subjects in which instruction was given in the
Mysteries.   Again he speaks of the High Priests, the

[1] *Ibid.*, ch. x.

[2] *Ibid.*, *The Martyrdom of Ignatius*, ch. i.

[3] *Ibid.*, *Epistle of Ignatius to the Ephesians*, ch. iii.

[4] *Ibid.*, ch. xii.

[5] *Ibid.*, *to the Trallians*, ch. v.

Hierophant, " to whom the holy of holies has been committed, and who alone has been entrusted with the secrets of God." [1]

We come next to St. Clement of Alexandria and his pupil Origen, the two writers of the second and third centuries who tell us most about the Mysteries in the Early Church; though the general atmosphere is full of mystic allusions, these two are clear and categorical in their statements that the Mysteries were a recognized institution.

Now St. Clement was a disciple of Pantaenus, and he speaks of him and of two others, said to be probably Tatian and Theodotus, as " preserving the tradition of the blessed doctrine derived directly from the holy Apostles, Peter, James, John and Paul," [2] his link with the Apostles themselves consisting thus of only one intermediary. He was the head of the Catechetical School of Alexandria in A.D. 189, and died about A.D. 220. Origen, born about A.D. 185, was his pupil, and he is, perhaps, the most learned of the Fathers, and a man of the rarest moral beauty. These are the witnesses from whom we receive the most important testimony as to the existence of definite Mysteries in the Early Church.

The *Stromata*, or Miscellanies, of St. Clement are our source of information about the Mysteries in his time. He himself speaks of these writings as a " miscellany of Gnostic notes, according to the true philosophy," [3] and

---

[1] *Ibid., to the Philadelphians*, ch. ix.

[2] Vol. IV. Clement of Alexandria, *Stromata*, bk. I.

[3] Vol. IV. *Stromata*, bk. I, ch. xxviii.

also describes them as memoranda of the teachings he had himself received from Pantaenus. The passage is instructive: " The Lord . . . allowed us to communicate of those divine Mysteries, and of that holy light, to those who are able to receive them. He did not certainly disclose to the many what did not belong to the many; but to the few to whom He knew that they belonged, who were capable of receiving and being moulded according to them. But secret things are entrusted to speech, not to writing, as in the case with God. And if one says [1] that it is written, ' There is nothing secret which shall not be revealed, nor hidden which shall not be disclosed,' let him also hear from us, that to him who hears secretly, even what is secret shall be manifested. This is what was predicted by this oracle. And to him who is able secretly to observe what is delivered to him, that which is veiled shall be disclosed as truth; and what is hidden to the many shall appear manifest to the few. . . . The Mysteries are delivered mystically, that what is spoken may be in the mouth of the speaker; rather not in his voice, but in his understanding. . . . The writing of these memoranda of mine, I well know, is weak when compared with that spirit, full of grace, which I was privileged to hear. But it will be an image to recall the archetype to him who was struck with the Thyrsus." The Thyrsus, we may here interject, was the wand borne by Initiates, and candidates were touched with it during the ceremony of Initiation. It had a

---

[1] It appears that even in those days there were some who objected to any truth being taught secretly!

mystic significance, symbolizing the spinal cord and the pineal gland in the Lesser Mysteries, and a Rod, known to Occultists in the Greater. To say, therefore, " to him who was struck with the Thyrsus " was exactly the same as to say, " to him who was initiated in the Mysteries." Clement proceeds: " We profess not to explain secret things sufficiently—far from it—but only to recall them to memory, whether we have forgot aught, or whether for the purpose of not forgetting. Many things, I well know, have escaped us, through length of time, that have dropped away unwritten. . . . There are then some things of which we have no recollection; for the power that was in the blessed men was great." A frequent experience of those taught by the Great Ones, for Their presence stimulates and renders active powers which are normally latent, and which the pupil, unassisted, cannot evoke. " There are also some things which remained unnoted long, which have now escaped; and others which are effaced, having faded away in the mind itself, since such a task is not easy to those not experienced; these I revive in my commentaries. Some things I purposely omit, in the exercise of a wise selection, afraid to write what I guarded against speaking; not grudging—for that were wrong—but fearing for my readers, lest they should stumble by taking them in a wrong sense; and, as the proverb says, we should be found ' reaching a sword to a child.' For it is impossible that what has been written should not escape (become known), although remaining unpublished by me. But being always revolved, using the one only voice, that of writing, they answer nothing to him that makes inquiries beyond what is written; for they require of necessity the aid of some one, either of him who wrote, or of some one else who has walked in his footsteps. Some things my treatise will hint; on some it will linger; some it will merely mention. It will try to speak imperceptibly, to exhibit secretly, and to demonstrate silently." [1]

This passage, if it stood alone, would suffice to establish the existence of a secret teaching in the Early Church. But it stands by no means alone. In chapter xii of this same Book I, headed, " The Mysteries of the Faith not to be divulged to all," Clement declares that, since others than the wise may see his work, " it is requisite, therefore, to hide in a Mystery the wisdom spoken, which the Son of God taught." Purified tongue of the speaker, purified ears of the hearer, these were necessary. " Such were the impediments in the way of my writing . . . the wise do not utter with their mouth what they reason in council. ' But what ye hear in the ear,' said the Lord, ' proclaim upon the houses ' bidding them receive the secret traditions of the true knowledge, and expound them aloft and conspicuously; and as we have heard in the ear, so to deliver them to whom it is requisite; but not enjoining us to communicate to all without distinction, what is said to them in parables. But there is only a delineation in the memoranda, which have the truth sown sparse and broadcast, that it may escape the notice of those who pick up seeds

[1] *Ibid.*, bk. I, ch. i.

like jackdaws; but when they find a good husbandman, each one of them will germinate and will produce corn."

Clement might have added that to " proclaim upon the houses " was to proclaim or expound in the assembly of the Perfect, the Initiate, and by no means to shout aloud to the man in the street.

Again he says that those who are " still blind and dumb, not having understanding, or the undazzled and keen vision of the contemplative soul . . . must stand outside of the divine choir. . . . Wherefore, in accordance with the method of concealment, the truly sacred Word, truly divine and most necessary for us, deposited in the shrine of truth, was by the Egyptians indicated by what were called among them *adyta*, and by the Hebrews by the veil. Only the consecrated . . . were allowed access to them. For Plato also thought it not lawful for ' the impure to touch the pure.' Thence the prophecies and oracles are spoken in enigmas, and the Mysteries are not exhibited incontinently to all and sundry, but only after certain purifications and previous instructions." [1] He then comments at great length on symbols, expounding Pythagorean, Hebrew, Egyptian,[2] and then remarks that the ignorant and unlearned man fails in understanding them. " But the Gnostic apprehends. Now then it is not wished that all things should be exposed indiscriminately to all and sundry, or the benefits of wisdom communicated to those who have not even in a dream been purified in soul (for it is not allowed to hand

[1] *Ibid.*, bk. V, ch. iv.
[2] *Ibid.*, ch. v-viii.

to every chance comer what has been procured with such laborious efforts); nor are the Mysteries of the Word to be expounded to the profane." The Pythagoreans and Plato, Zeno, and Aristotle had exoteric and esoteric teachings. The philosophers established the Mysteries, for " was it not more beneficial for the holy and blessed contemplation of realities to be concealed? " [1] The Apostles also approved of " veiling the Mysteries of the Faith," " for there is an instruction to the perfect," alluded to in Colossians i, 9-11 and 25-27. " So that, on the one hand, then, there are the Mysteries which were hid till the time of the Apostles, and were delivered by them as they were received from the Lord and concealed in the Old Testament, were manifested to the saints. And, on the other hand, there is ' the riches of the glory of the mystery in the Gentiles,' which is faith and hope in Christ; which in another place he has called the ' foundation.' " He quotes St. Paul to show that this " knowledge belongs not to all," and says, referring to Heb. v and vi, that " there were certainly among the Hebrews, some things delivered unwritten "; and then refers to St. Barnabas, who speaks of God, " who has put into our hearts wisdom and the understanding of His secrets," and says that " it is but for few to comprehend these things," as showing a " trace of Gnostic tradition." " Wherefore instruction, which reveals hidden things, is called illumination, as it is the teacher only who uncovers the lid of the ark." [2]

[1] *Ibid.*, ch. ix.
[2] *Ibid.*, bk. V. ch. x.

Further referring to St. Paul, he comments on his remark to the Romans that he will " come in the fulness
of the blessing of Christ," [1] and says that he thus desig-
nates " the spiritual gift and the Gnostic interpretation,
which being present he desires to impart to them present as the fulness of Christ, according to the revelation
of the Mystery sealed in the ages of eternity, but now
manifested by the prophetic Scriptures [2]. . . . But only
to a few of them is shown what those things are which
are contained in the Mystery. Rightly, then, Plato, in
the epistles, treating of God, says: ' We must speak in
enigmas; that should the tablet come by any mischance
on its leaves either by sea or land, he who reads may
remain ignorant.' " [3]

After much examination of Greek writers, and an investigation into philosophy, St. Clement declares that the
Gnosis "imparted and revealed by the Son of God, is
wisdom. . . . And the Gnosis itself is that which has
descended by transmission to a few, having been im-
ported unwritten by the Apostles." [4] A very long exposition of the life of the Gnostic, the Initiate, is given,
and St. Clement concludes it by saying: " Let the specimen suffice to those who have ears. For it is not required
to unfold the mystery, but only to indicate what is

---

[1] *Loc. cit.*, xv, 29.

[2] *Ibid.*, xvi, 25-26; the version quoted differs in words, but not
in meaning, from the English Authorised Version.

[3] *Stromata*, bk. V, ch. x.

[4] *Ibid.*, bk. VI, ch. vii.

sufficient for those who are partakers in knowledge to
bring it to mind." [1]

Regarding Scripture as consisting of allegories and
symbols, and as hiding the sense in order to stimulate
inquiry and to preserve the ignorant from danger,[2]
St. Clement naturally confined the higher instruction to
the learned. " Our Gnostic will be deeply learned," [3]
he says. " Now the Gnostic must be erudite." [4] Those
who had acquired readiness by previous training could
master the deeper knowledge, for though " a man can
be a believer without learning, so also we assert that it
is impossible for a man without learning to comprehend
the things which are declared in the faith." [5] " Some
who think themselves naturally gifted, do not wish to
touch either philosophy or logic; nay more, they do not
wish to learn natural science. They demand bare faith
alone. . . . So also I call him truly learned who brings
everything to bear on the truth—so that, from geometry, and music, and grammar, and philosophy itself,
culling what is useful, he guards the faith against assault.
. . . How necessary is it for him who desires to be
partaker of the power of God, to treat of intellectual
subjects by philosophizing." [6] " The Gnostic avails
himself of branches of learning as auxiliary preparatory

[1] *Ibid.*, bk. VII, ch. xiv.
[2] *Ibid.*, bk. VI, ch. xv.
[3] *Ibid.*, bk. VI, ch. x.
[4] *Ibid.*, bk. VI. ch. vii.
[5] *Ibid.*, bk. I, ch. vi.
[6] *Ibid.*, ch. ix.

exercise." [1] So far was St. Clement from thinking that the teaching of Christianity should be measured by the ignorance of the unlearned. " He who is conversant with all kinds of wisdom will be pre-eminently a Gnostic." [2] Thus while he welcomed the ignorant and the sinner, and found in the Gospel what was suited to their needs, he considered that only the learned and the pure were fit candidates for the Mysteries. " The Apostle, in contradistinction to Gnostic perfection, calls the common faith *the foundation*, and sometimes *milk*." [3] But on that foundation the edifice of the Gnostic was to be raised, and the food of men was to succeed that of babes. There is nothing of harshness nor of contempt in the distinction he draws, but only a calm and wise recognition of the facts.

Even the well-prepared candidate, the learned and trained pupil, could only hope to advance step by step in the profound truths unveiled in the Mysteries. This appears clearly in his comments on the vision of Hermas, in which he also throws out some hints on methods of reading occult works. " Did not the Power also, that appeared to Hermas in the Vision, in the form of the Church, give for transcription the book which she wished to be made known to the elect? And this, he says, he transcribed to the letter, without finding how to complete the syllables. And this signified that the Scripture is clear to all, when taken according to base

[1] *Ibid.*, bk. VI, ch. x.

[2] *Ibid.*, bk. I, ch. xiii.

[3] Vol. XII, *Stromata*, bk. V, ch. iv.

reading; and that this is the faith which occupies the place of the rudiments. Wherefore also the figurative expression is employed, 'reading according to the letter,' while we understand that the gnostic unfolding of Scriptures, when faith has already reached an advanced state, is likened to reading according to the syllables. . . . Now that the Saviour has taught the Apostles, the unwritten rendering of the written (scriptures) has been handed down also to us, inscribed by the power of God on hearts new, according to the renovation of the book. Thus those of highest repute among the Greeks dedicate the fruit of the pomegranate to Hermes, who they say is speech, on account of its interpretation. For speech conceals much. . . . That it is therefore not only to those who read simply that the acquisition of the truth is so difficult, but that not even to those whose prerogative the knowledge of the truth is, is the contemplation of it vouchsafed all at once, the history of Moses teaches; until accustomed to gaze, as the Hebrews on the glory of Moses, and the prophets of Israel on the visions of angels, so we also become able to look the splendours of truth in the face." [1]

Yet more references might be given, but these should suffice to establish the fact that St. Clement knew of, had been initiated into, and wrote for the benefit of those who had also been initiated into, the Mysteries in the Church.

The next witness is his pupil Origen, that most shining light of learning, courage, sanctity, devotion, meekness

[1] *Ibid.*, bk. VI, ch. xv.

and zeal, whose works remain as mines of gold wherein the student may dig for the treasures of wisdom.

In his famous controversy with Celsus attacks were made on Christianity which drew out a defence of the Christian position in which frequent references were made to the secret teachings.[1]

Celsus had alleged, as a matter of attack, that Christianity was a secret system, and Origen traverses this by saying that while certain doctrines were secret, many others were public, and that this system of exoteric and esoteric teachings, adopted in Christianity, was also in general use among philosophers. The reader should note, in the following passage, the distinction drawn between the resurrection of Jesus, regarded in a historical light, and the " mystery of the resurrection."

" Moreover, since he (Celsus) frequently calls the Christian doctrine a secret system [of belief], we must confute him on this point also, since almost the entire world is better acquainted with what Christians preach than with the favorite opinions of philosophers. For who is ignorant of the statement that Jesus was born of a virgin, and that He was crucified, and that His resurrection is an article of faith among many, and that a general judgment is announced to come, in which the wicked are to be punished according to their deserts, and the righteous to be duly rewarded? And yet the Mystery of the resurrection, not being understood, is made a subject of ridicule among unbelievers. In these

[1] Book I, of *Against Celsus* is found in Vol. X of the Ante-Nicene Library. The remaining books are in Vol. XXIII.

circumstances, to speak of the Christian doctrine as a *secret* system, is altogether absurd. But that there should be certain doctrines, not made known to the multitude, which are (revealed) after the exoteric ones have been taught, is not a peculiarity of Christianity alone, but also of philosophic systems, in which certain truths are exoteric and others esoteric. Some of the hearers of Pythagoras were content with his *ipse dixit*; while others were taught in secret those doctrines which were not deemed fit to be communicated to profane and insufficiently prepared ears. Moreover, all the Mysteries that are celebrated everywhere throughout Greece and barbarous countries, although held in secret, have no discredit thrown upon them, so that it is in vain he endeavours to calumniate the secret doctrines of Christianity, seeing that he does not correctly understand its nature." [1]

It is impossible to deny that, in this important passage, Origen distinctly places the Christian Mysteries in the same category as those of the Pagan world, and claims that what is not regarded as a discredit to other religions should not form a subject of attack when found in Christianity.

Still writing against Celsus, he declares that the secret teachings of Jesus were preserved in the Church, and refers specifically to the explanations that He gave to His disciples of His parables, in answering Celsus' comparison of " the inner Mysteries of the Church of God " with the Egyptian worship of Animals. " I have not

[1] Vol. X. *Origen Against Celsus*, bk. I, ch. vii.

yet spoken of the observance of all that is written in the Gospels, each one of which contains much doctrine difficult to be understood, not merely by the multitude, but even by certain of the more intelligent, including a very profound explanation of the parables which Jesus delivered to 'those without,' while reserving the exhibition of their full meaning for those who had passed beyond the stage of exoteric teaching, and who came to Him privately in the house. And when he comes to understand it, he will admire the reason why some are said to be 'without,' and others 'in the house.' " [1]

And he refers guardedly to the " mountain " which Jesus ascended, from which He came down again to help " those who were unable to follow Him whither His disciples went." [1] The allusion is to " the Mountain of Initiation," a well-known mystical phrase, as Moses also made the Tabernacle after the pattern " showed thee in the mount." [2] Origen refers to it again later, saying that Jesus showed himself to be very different in His real appearance when on the " Mountain," from what those saw who could not " follow Him so high." [3]

So also, in his commentary on the Gospel of Matthew, chap. xv, dealing with the episode of the Syro-Phoenician woman, Origen remarks: " And perhaps also, of the words of Jesus there are some loaves which

[1] Vol. X. *Origen Against Celsus*, bk. I, ch. vii.
[2] Ex. xxv, 40, xxvi 30, and compare with Heb. viii, 5, and ix, 25.
[3] *Origen Against Celsus*, bk. IV, ch. xvi.

it is possible to give to the more rational, as to children, only. . ."

Celsus complaining that sinners were brought into the Church, Origen answers that the Church had medicine for those that were sick, but also the study and the knowledge of divine things for those who were in health. Sinners were taught not to sin, and only when it was seen that progress had been made, and men were " purified by the Word," then, and not before, " do we invite them to participation in our Mysteries. For we speak wisdom among them that are perfect." [1] Sinners came to be healed: " For there are in the divinity of the Word some helps towards the cure of those who are sick. . . . Others, again, which to the pure in soul and body exhibit the ' revelation of the Mystery, which was kept secret since the world began, but now is made manifest by the Scriptures of the prophets,' and ' by the appearing of our Lord Jesus Christ,' which ' appearing ' is manifested to each one of those who are perfect, and which enlightens the reason in the true knowledge of things." [2] Such appearances of divine Beings took place, we have seen, in the Pagan Mysteries, and those of the Church had equally glorious visitants. " God the Word," he says, " was sent as a physician to sinners, but as a Teacher of Divine Mysteries to those who are already pure, and who sin no more." [3] " Wisdom will not enter into the soul of a base man, nor dwell in a body

[1] *Origen Against Celsus*, bk. III, ch. lix.
[2] *Ibid.*, ch. lxi.
[3] *Ibid.*, ch. lxii.

that is involved in sin "; hence these higher teachings are given only to those who are " athletes in piety and in every virtue."

Christians did not admit the impure to this knowledge, but said: " Whoever has clean hands, and, therefore, lifts up holy hands to God . . . let him come to us. . . . Whoever is pure not only from all defilement, but from what are regarded as lesser transgressions, let him be boldly initiated in the Mysteries of Jesus, which properly are made known only to the holy and the pure." Hence also, ere the ceremony of Initiation began, he who acts as Initiator, according to the precepts of Jesus, the Hierophant, made the significant proclamation " to those who have been purified in heart: he, whose soul has, for a long time, been conscious of no evil, especially since he yielded himself to the healing of the Word, let such a one hear the doctrines which were spoken in private by Jesus to His genuine disciples." This was the .opening of the " initiating of those who were already purified into the sacred Mysteries." [1] Such only might learn the realities of the unseen worlds, and might enter into the sacred precincts where, as of old, angels were the teachers, and where knowledge was given by sight and not only by words. It is impossible not to be struck with the different tone of these Christians from that of their modern successors. With them perfect purity of life, the practice of virtue, the fulfilling of the divine Law in every detail of outer conduct, the perfection of righteousness, were—as with the Pagans—

[1] *Origen Against Celsus*, bk. III, ch. lx.

only the beginning of the way instead of the end. Nowadays religion is considered to have gloriously accomplished its object when it has made the Saint; then, it was to the Saints that it devoted its highest energies, and, taking the pure in heart, it led them to the Beatific Vision.

The same fact of secret teaching comes out again, when Origen is discussing the arguments of Celsus as to the wisdom of retaining ancestral customs, based on the belief that " the various quarters of the earth were from the beginning allotted to different superintending Spirits, and were thus distributed among certain governing Powers, and in this way the administration of the world is carried on." [1]

Origen, having animadverted on the deductions of Celsus, proceeds: " But as we think it likely that some of those who are accustomed to deeper investigation will fall in with this treatise, let us venture to lay down some considerations of a profounder kind, conveying a mystical and secret view respecting the original distribution of the various quarters of the earth among different superintending Spirits." [2] He says that Celsus has misunderstood the deeper reasons relating to the arrangement of terrestrial affairs, some of which are even touched upon in Grecian history. Then he quotes Deut., xxxii, 8-9: " When the Most High divided the nations, when he dispersed the sons of Adam, He set the bounds of the people according to the number of

[1] Vol. XXIII, *Origen Against Celsus*, bk. V, ch. xxv.
[2] *Ibid.*, ch. xxviii

the Angels of God; and the Lord's portion was his people Jacob, and Israel the cord of his inheritance." This is the wording of the Septuagint, not that of the English authorised version, but it is very suggestive of the title, the " Lord " being regarded as that of the Ruling Angel of the Jews only, and not of the " Most High," *i.e.*, God. This view has disappeared, from ignorance, and hence the impropriety of many of the statements referring to the " Lord," when they are transferred to the" Most High," *e.g.*, Judges, i, 19.

Origen then relates the history of the Tower of Babel, and continues: " But on these subjects much, and that of a mystical kind, might be said; in keeping with which is the following: ' It is good to keep close the secret of a king,' Tobit, xii, 7, in order that the doctrine of the entrance of souls into bodies (not, however, that of the transmigration from one body into another) may not be thrown before the common understanding, nor what is holy given to the dogs, nor pearls be cast before swine. For such a procedure would be impious, being equivalent to a betrayal of the mysterious declarations of God's wisdom. . . . It is sufficient, however, to represent in the style of a historic narrative what is intended to convey a secret meaning in the garb of history, that those who have the capacity may work out for themselves all that relates to the subject." [1]   He then expounds more fully the Tower of Babel story, and writes: " Now, in the next place, if any one has the capacity let him understand that in what assumes the form of

[1] Vol. XXIII, *Origen Against Celsus*, bk. V, ch. xxix.

history, and which contains some things that are literally true, while yet it conveys a deeper meaning. . . ." [1]

After endeavouring to show that the " Lord " was more powerful than the other superintending Spirits of the different quarters of the earth, and that he sent his people forth to be punished by living under the dominion of the other powers, and afterwards reclaimed them with all of the less favoured nations who could be drawn in, Origen concludes by saying: " As we have previously observed, these remarks are to be understood as being made by us with a concealed meaning, by way of pointing out the mistakes of those who assert . . ." [2] as did Celsus.

After remarking that " the object of Christianity is that we should become wise," [3] Origen proceeds: " If you come to the books written after the time of Jesus, you will find that those multitudes of believers who hear the parables are, as it were, ' without,' and worthy only of exoteric doctrines, while the disciples learn in private the explanation of the parables. For, privately, to his own disciples did Jesus open up all things, esteeming above the multitudes those who desired to know His wisdom. And He promises to those who believe on Him to send them wise men and scribes. . . . And Paul also in the catalogue of ' Charismata ' bestowed by God, placed first ' the Word of wisdom,' and second, as being inferior to it, ' the word of knowledge,' but third,

[1] Vol. XXIII, *Origen Against Celsus*, bk. V, ch. xxix.
[2] *Ibid.*, ch. xxxii.
[3] *Ibid.*, ch. xlv.

and lower down, 'faith.' And because he regarded 'the Word' as higher than miraculous powers, he for that reason places 'working of miracles' and 'gifts of healings' in a lower place than gifts of the Word." [1]

The Gospel truly helped the ignorant, " but it is no hindrance to the knowledge of God, but an assistance, to have been educated, and to have studied the best opinions, and to be wise." [2]   As for the unintelligent, " I endeavour to improve such also to the best of my ability, although I would not desire to build up the Christian community out of such materials. For I seek in reference those who are more clever and acute, because they are able to comprehend the meaning of the hard sayings." [3]   Here we have plainly stated the ancient Christian idea, entirely at one with the considerations submitted in Chapter I of this book.

It is for these that he takes much pains to show that the Jewish and Christian Scriptures have hidden meanings, veiled under stories the outer meaning of which repels them as absurd, alluding to the serpent and the tree of life, and " the other statements which follow, which might of themselves lead a candid reader to see that all these things had, not inappropriately, an allegorical meaning." [4]   Many chapters are devoted to these allegorical and mystical meanings, hidden beneath

[1] Vol. XXIII, *Origen Against Celsus*, bk. V, ch. xlvi.
[2] *Ibid.*, chs. xlvii-liv.
[3] *Ibid.*, ch. lxxiv.
[4] *Ibid.*, bk. IV, ch. xxxix.

the words of the Old and New Testaments, and he alleges that Moses, like the Egyptians, gave histories with concealed meanings.[1] " He who deals candidly with histories "—this is Origen's general canon of interpretation—" and would wish to keep himself also from being imposed on by them, will exercise his judgment as to what statements he will give his assent to, and what he will accept figuratively, seeking to discover the meaning of the authors of such inventions, and from what statements he will withhold his beliefs, as having been written for the gratification of certain individuals. And we have said this by way of anticipation respecting the whole history related in the Gospels concerning Jesus." [2] A great part of his Fourth Book is taken up with illustrations of the mystical explanations of the Scripture stories, and anyone who wishes to pursue the subject can read through it.

In the *De Principiis* Origen gives it as the received teaching of the Church " that the Scriptures were written by the Spirit of God, and have a meaning, not only such as is apparent at first sight, but also another, which escapes the notice of most. For those [words] which are written are the forms of certain Mysteries, and the images of divine things. Respecting which there is one opinion throughout the whole Church, that the whole law is indeed spiritual; but that the spiritual meaning which the law conveys is not known to all, but to those only on whom the grace of the Holy Spirit is bestowed

[1] Vol. X, *Origen Against Celsus*, bk. I, ch. xvii and others.
[2] *Ibid.*, bk. I, ch. xlii.

in the word of wisdom and knowledge." [1] Those who remember what has already been quoted will see in the " Word of wisdom " and " the word of knowl- edge " the two typical mystical instructions, the spiritual and the intellectual.

In the Fourth Book of *De Principiis*, Origen explains at length his views on the interpretation of Scripture. It has a " body," which is the " common and historical sense "; a " soul," a figurative meaning to be discovered by the exercise of the intellect; and a " spirit," an inner and divine sense, to be known only by those who have " the mind of Christ." He considers that incongruous and impossible things are introduced into the history to arouse an intelligent reader, and compel him to search for a deeper explanation, while simple people would read on without appreciating the difficulties. [2]

Cardinal Newman, in his *Arians of the Fourth Cen- tury*, has some interesting remarks on the *Disciplina Arcani*, but, with the deeply-rooted ingrained scepticism of the nineteenth century, he cannot believe to the full in the " riches of the glory of the Mystery," or probably never for a moment conceived the possibility of the existence of such splendid realities. Yet he was a be- liever in Jesus, and the words of the promise of Jesus were clear and definite: " I will not leave you comfort- less; I will come to you. Yet a little while, and the world seeth me to more; but ye see me: because I live, ye shall live also. At that day ye shall know that I am

[1] Vol. X. *De Principiis*, Preface, p. 8.
[2] *Ibid.*, ch. i.

in my Father, and ye in me, and I in you." [1] The promise was amply redeemed, for He came to them and taught them in His Mysteries; therein they saw Him, though the world saw Him no more, and they knew the Christ as in them, and their life as Christ's.

Cardinal Newman recognizes a secret tradition, handed down from the Apostles, but he considers that it consisted of Christian doctrines, later divulged, forgetting that those who were told that they were not yet fit to receive it were not heathen, nor even catechumens under instruction, but full communicating members of the Christian Church. Thus he states that this secret tradition was later " authoritatively divulged and perpetuated in the form of symbols," and was embodied " in the creeds of the early Councils." [2] But as the doctrines in the creeds are to be found clearly stated in the Gospels and Epistles, this position is wholly untenable, all these having been already divulged to the world at large; and in all of them the members of the Church were certainly thoroughly instructed. The repeated statements as to secrecy become meaningless if thus explained. The Cardinal, however, says that whatever " has not been thus authenticated, whether it was prophetical information or comment on the past dispensations, is, from the circumstances of the case, lost to the Church." [3] That is very probably, in fact, certainly, true, so far as the Church is concerned, but it is none the less recoverable.

[1] St. John, xiv, 18-20.
[2] *Loc. cit.*, ch. i, Sec. III, p. 55.
[3] *Ibid.*, pp. 55, 56.

6

Commenting on Irenaeus, who in his work *Against Heresies* lays much stress on the existence of an Apostolic Tradition in the Church, the Cardinal writes: " He then proceeds to speak of the clearness and cogency of the traditions preserved in the Church, as containing that true wisdom of the perfect, of which St. Paul speaks, and to which the Gnostics pretended. And, indeed, without formal proofs of the existence and authority in primitive times of an Apostolic Tradition, it is plain that there must have been such a tradition, granting that the Apostles conversed, and their friends had memories, like other men. It is quite inconceivable that they should not have been led to arrange the series of revealed doctrines more systematically than they record them in Scripture, as soon as their converts became exposed to the attacks and misrepresentations of heretics, unless they were forbidden to do so, a supposition which cannot be maintained. Their statements thus occasioned would be preserved as a matter of course; together with those other secret but less important truths, to which St. Paul seems to allude, and which the early writers more or less acknowledge, whether concerning the types of the Jewish Church, or the prospective fortunes of the Christian. And such recollections of apostolical teaching would evidently be binding on the faith of those who were instructed in them; unless it can be supposed that, though coming from inspired teachers, they were not of divine origin." [1]   In a part of the section dealing with the allegorizing method, he writes in reference to

[1] *Ibid.*, pp. 54, 55.

the sacrifice of Isaac, etc., as "typical of the New Testament revelation ": " In corroboration of this remark, let it be observed, that there seems to have been [1] in the Church a traditionary explanation of these historical types, derived from the Apostles, but kept among the secret doctrines, as being dangerous to the majority of hearers; and certainly St. Paul, in the Epistle to the Hebrews, affords us an instance of such a tradition, both as existing and as secret (even though it be shown to be of Jewish origin), when, first checking himself and questioning his brethren's faith, he communicates, not without hesitation, the evangelical scope of the account of Melchisedec, as introduced into the book of Genesis." [2]

The social and political convulsions that accompanied its dying, now began to torture the vast frame of the Roman Empire, and even the Christians were caught up in the whirlpool of selfish warring interests. We still find scattered references to special knowledge imparted to the leaders and teachers of the Church, knowledge of the heavenly hierarchies, instructions given by angels, and so on. But the lack of suitable pupils caused the Mysteries to be withdrawn as an institution publicly known to exist, and teaching was given more and more secretly to those rarer and rarer souls, who by learning, purity and devotion showed themselves capable of

[1] " Seems to have been " is a somewhat weak expression, after what is said by Clement and Origen, of which some specimens are given in the text.

[2] *Ibid.*, p. 62.

receiving it. No longer were schools to be found wherein the preliminary teachings were given, and with the disappearance of these the " door was shut."

Two streams may nevertheless be tracked through Christendom, streams which had as their source the vanished Mysteries. One was the stream of mystic learning, flowing from the Wisdom, the Gnosis, imparted in the Mysteries; the other was the stream of mystic contemplation, equally part of the Gnosis, leading to the ecstasy, to spiritual vision. This latter, however, divorced from knowledge, rarely attained the true ecstasies, and tended either to run riot in the lower regions of the invisible worlds, or to lose itself amid a variegated crowd of subtle superphysical forms, visible as objective appearances to the inner vision—prematurely forced by fastings, vigils, and strained attention— but mostly born of the thoughts and emotions of the seer. Even when the forms observed were not externalized thoughts, they were seen through a distorting atmosphere of preconceived ideas and beliefs, and were thus rendered largely unreliable. None the less, some of the visions were verily of heavenly things, and Jesus truly appeared from time to time to His devoted lovers, and angels would sometimes brighten with their presence the call of monk and nun, the solitude of rapt devotee and patient seeker after God. To deny the possibility of such experiences would be to strike at the very root of that " which has been most surely believed " in all religions, and is known to all Occultists—the intercommunication between Spirits veiled in flesh and those clad in subtler vestures, the touching of mind with mind across the barriers of matter, the unfolding of the Divinity in man, the sure knowledge of a life beyond the gates of death.

Glancing down the centuries we find no time in which Christendom was left wholly devoid of mysteries. " It was probably about the end of the 5th century, just as ancient philosophy was dying out in the Schools of Athens, that the speculative philosophy of Neo-platonism made a definite lodgement in Christian thought through the literary forgeries of the Pseudo-Dionysius. The doctrines of Christianity were by that time so firmly established that the Church could look upon a symbolical or mystical interpretation of them without anxiety. The author of the *Theologica Mystica* and the other works ascribed to the Areopagite proceeds, therefore, to develop the doctrines of Proclus with very little modification into a system of esoteric Christianity. God is the nameless and supra-essential One, elevated above goodness itself. Hence ' negative theology,' which ascends from the creature to God by dropping one after another every determinate predicate, leads us nearest to the truth. The return to God is the consummation of all things and the goal indicated by Christian teaching. The same doctrines were preached with more of churchly fervour by Maximus, the Confessor, (580-622). Maximus represents almost the last speculative activity of the Greek Church, but the influence of the Pseudo-Dionysian writing was transmitted to the West in the ninth century by Erigena, in whose speculative spirit both the scholasticism and the mysticism of the Middle Ages have their rise. Erigena translated Dionysius into Latin along with the commentaries of Maximus, and his system is essentially based upon theirs. The negative theology is adopted, and God is stated to be predicateless Being, above all categories, and therefore not improperly called Nothing [*query*, No-Thing]. Out of this Nothing or incomprehensible essence the world of ideas or primordial causes is eternally created. This is the Word or Son of God, in whom all things exist, so far as they have substantial existence. All existence is a theophany, and as God is the beginning of all things, so also is He the end. Erigena teaches the restitution of all things under the form of the Dionysian *adunatio* or *deificatio*. These are the permanent outlines of what may be called the philosophy of mysticism in Christian times, and it is remarkable with how little variation they are repeated from age to age." [1]

In the eleventh century Bernard of Clairvaux (A.D. 1091-1153) and Hugo of St. Victor carry on the mystic tradition, with Richard of St. Victor in the following century, and St. Bonaventura the Seraphic Doctor, and the great St. Thomas Aquinas (A.D. 1227-1274) in the thirteenth. Thomas Aquinas dominates the Europe of the Middle Ages, by his force of character no less than by his learning and piety. He asserts " Revelation " as one source of knowledge, Scripture and tradition being the two channels in which it runs, and the influences, seen in his writings, of the Pseudo-Dionysius links him

[1] Article on " Mysticism." *Encyc. Brit.*

to the Neo-platonists. The second source is Reason,
and here the channels are the Platonic philosophy and
the methods of Aristotle—the latter an alliance that did
Christianity no good, for Aristotle became an obstacle
to the advance of the higher thought, as was made manifest in the struggles of Giordano Bruno, the Pythagorean. Thomas Aquinas was canonized in A.D. 1323,
and the great Dominican remains as a type of the union
of theology and philosophy—the aim of his life. These
belong to the great Church of western Europe, vindi-
cating her claim to be regarded as the transmitter of the
holy torch of mystic learning. Around her there also
sprang up many sects, deemed heretical, yet containing
true traditions of the sacred secret learning, the Cathari
and many others, persecuted by a Church jealous of her
authority, and fearing lest the holy pearls should pass
into profane custody. In this century also St. Elizabeth
of Hungary shines out with sweetness and purity, while
Eckhart (A.D. 1260-1329) proves himself a worthy in-
heritor of the Alexandrian Schools. Eckhart taught
that " the Godhead is the absolute Essence (*Wesen*),
unknowable not only by man but also by Itself;
It is darkness and absolute indeterminateness, *'Nicht*
in contrast to *Icht*, or definite and knowable
existence. Yet It is the potentiality of all things,
and Its nature is, in a triadic process, to come to
consciousness of Itself as the triune God. Creation
is not a temporal act, but an eternal necessity,
of the divine nature. I am as necessary to God,
Eckhart is fond of saying, as God is necessary to

me. In my knowledge and love God knows and loves Himself." [1]

Eckhart is followed, in the fourteenth century, by John Tauler, and Nicolas of Basel, " the Friend of God in the Oberland." From these sprang up the Society of the Friends of God, true mystics and followers of the old tradition. Mead remarks that Thomas Aquinas, Tauler and Eckhart followed the Pseudo-Dionysius, who followed Plotinus, Iamblichus, and Proclus, who in turn followed Plato and Pythagoras.[2] So linked together are the followers of the Wisdom in all ages. It was probably a " Friend " who was the author of *Die Deutsche Theologie*, a book of mystical devotion, which had the curious fortune of being approved by Staupitz, the Vicar-General of the Augustinian Order, who recommended it to Luther, and by Luther himself, who published it in A.D. 1516 as a book which should rank immediately after the Bible and the writings of St. Augustine of Hippo. Another " Friend " was Ruysbroeck to whose influence with Groot was due the founding of the Brethren of the Common Lot or Common Life—a Society that must remain ever memorable, as it numbered among its members that prince of mystics, Thomas à Kempis (A.D. 1380-1471), the author of the immortal *Imitation of Christ*.

In the fifteenth century the more purely intellectual side of mysticism comes out more strongly than the ecstatic—so dominant in these societies of the

[1] Article " Mysticism." *Encyclopaedia Britannica.*
[2] *Orpheus*, pp. 53, 54.

fourteenth—and we have Cardinal Nicolas of Cusa, with Giordano Bruno, the martyred knight-errant of philosophy, and Paracelsus, the much-slandered scientist who drew his knowledge directly from the original eastern fountain, instead of through Greek channels.

The sixteenth century saw the birth of Jacob Böhme (A.D. 1575-1624), the " inspired cobbler," an Initiate in obscuration truly, sorely persecuted by unenlightened men; and then too came St. Teresa, the much-oppressed and suffering Spanish mystic; and St. John of the Cross, a burning flame of intense devotion; and St. Francois de Sales. Wise was Rome in canonizing these, wiser than the Reformation that persecuted Böhme, but the spirit of the Reformation was ever intensely anti-mystical, and wherever its breath hath passed the fair flowers of mysticism have withered as under the sirocco.

Rome, however, who, though she canonized Teresa dead, had sorely harried her while living—did ill with Mme. de Guyon (A.D. 1648-1717), a true mystic, and with Miguel de Molinos, (1627-1696), worthy to sit near St. John of the Cross, who carried on in the seventeenth century the high devotion of the mystic, turned into a peculiarly passive form—the Quietist.

In this same century arose the school of Platonists in Cambridge, of whom Henry More (A.D. 1614-1687) may serve as salient example; also Thomas Vaughan, and Robert Fludd the Rosicrucian; and there is formed also the Philadelphian Society, and we see William Law (A.D. 1686-1761) active in the eighteenth century, and overlapping St. Martin (A.D. 1743-1803), whose writing have fascinated so many nineteenth century students.[1]

Nor should we omit Christian Rosenkreutz (d. A.D. 1484), whose mystic Society of the Rosy Cross, appearing in 1614, held true knowledge, and whose spirit was reborn in the " Comte de St. Germain," the mysterious figure that appears and disappears through the gloom, lit by lurid flashes, of the closing eighteenth century. Mystics too were some of the Quakers, the much-persecuted sect of Friends, seeking the illumination of the Inner Light, and listening ever for the Inner Voice. And many another mystic was there, " of whom the world was not worthy," like the wholly delightful and wise Mother Juliana of Norwich, of the fourteenth century, jewels of Christendom, too little known, but justifying Christianity to the world.

Yet, as we salute reverently these Children of the Light, scattered over the centuries, we are forced to recognize in them the absence of that union of acute intellect and high devotion which were welded together by the training of the Mysteries, and while we marvel that they soared so high, we cannot but wish that their rare gifts had been developed under that magnificent *disciplina arcani*.

Alphonse Louis Constant, better known under his pseudonym, Éliphas Lévi, has put rather well the loss of the Mysteries, and the need for their reinstitution.

[1] Obligation must be here acknowledged to the article " Mysticism," in the *Encyc. Brit.*, though that publication is by no means responsible for the opinions expressed.

" A great misfortune befell Christianity.   The betrayal of the Mysteries by the false Gnostics—for the Gnostics, that is, *those who know*, were the Initiates of primitive Christianity—caused the Gnosis to be rejected, and alienated the Church from the supreme truths of the Kabbala, which contain all the secrets of transcendental theology. . . . Let the most absolute science, let the highest reason, become once more the patrimony of the leaders of the people; let the sacerdotal art and the royal art take the double sceptre of antique initiations, and the social world will once more issue from its chaos. Burn the holy images no longer; demolish the temples no more; temples and images are necessary for men; but drive the hirelings from the house of prayer; let the blind be no longer leaders of the blind, reconstruct the hierarchy of intelligence and holiness, and recognize only those who know as the teachers of those who believe." [1]

Will the Churches of today again take up the mystic teaching, the Lesser Mysteries, and so prepare their children for the re-establishment of the Greater Mysteries, again drawing down the Angels as Teachers, and having as Hierophant the Divine Master, Jesus? On the answer to that question depends the future of Christianity.

[1] *The Mysteries of Magic.* Trans., by A. E. Waite, pp. 58 and 60

CHAPTER IV

THE HISTORICAL CHRIST

WE have already spoken, in the first chapter, on the identities existing in all the religions of the world, and we have seen that out of a study of these identities, in beliefs, symbolisms, rites, ceremonies, histories, and commemorative festivals, has arisen a modern school which relates the whole of these to a common source in human ignorance, and in a primitive explanation of natural phenomena. From these identities have been drawn weapons for the stabbing of each religion in turn, and the most effective attacks on Christianity and on the historical existence of its Founder have been armed from this source. On entering now on the study of the life of the Christ, of the rites of Christianity, its sacraments, its doctrines, it would be fatal to ignore the facts marshalled by comparative mythologists. Rightly understood, they may be made serviceable instead of mischievous. We have seen that the Apostles and their successors dealt very freely with the Old Testament as having an allegorical and mystic sense far more important than the historical, though by no means negating it, and that they did not scruple to teach the instructed believer that some of the stories that were apparently historical were really purely allegorical. Nowhere, perhaps, is it more necessary to understand this than when we are studying the story of Jesus, surnamed the Christ, for when we do not disentangle the intertwisted threads, and see where symbols have been taken as events, allegories as histories, we lose most of the instructiveness of the narrative and much of its rarest beauty. We cannot too much insist on the fact that Christianity gains, it does not lose, when knowledge is added to faith and virtue, according to the apostolic injunction.[1] Men fear that Christianity will be weakened when reason studies it, and that it is "dangerous" to admit that events thought to be historical have the deeper significance of the mythical or mystical meaning. It is, on the contrary, strengthened, and the student finds with joy, that the pearl of great price shines with a purer, clearer lustre when the coating of ignorance is removed and its many colours are seen.

There are two schools of thought at the present time, who dispute over the story of the great Hebrew Teacher. According to one school there is nothing at all in the accounts of His life save myths and legends—myths and legends that were given as explanations of certain natural phenomena, survivals of a pictorial way of teaching certain facts of nature, of impressing on the minds of the uneducated certain grand classifications of natural events that were important in themselves, and that lent themselves to moral instruction. Those who endorse this view form

[1] II. St. Peter, i, 5.

a well-defined school to which belong many men of high education and strong intelligence, and around them gather crowds of the less instructed, who emphasize with crude vehemence the more destructive elements in their pronouncements. This school is opposed by that of the believers in orthodox Christianity, who declare that the whole story of Jesus is history, unadulterated by legend or myth. They maintain that this history is nothing more than the history of the life of a man born some nineteen centuries ago in Palestine, who passed through all the experiences set down in the Gospels, and they deny that the story has any significance beyond that of a divine and human life. These two schools stand in direct antagonism, one asserting that everything is legend, the other declaring that everything is history. Between them lie many phases of opinion which regard the life-story as partly legendary and partly historical, but offer no definite and rational method of interpretation, no adequate explanation of the complex whole. And we also find, within the limits of the Christian Church, a large and ever-increasing number of faithful and devout Christians of refined intelligence, men and women who are earnest in their faith and religious in their aspirations, but who see in the Gospel story more than the history of a single divine Man. They allege—defending their position from the received Scriptures—that the story of the Christ has a deeper and more significant meaning than lies on the surface; while they maintain the historical character of Jesus, they at the same time declare that THE CHRIST is more than the man Jesus, and has a mystical meaning. In support of this contention they point to such phrases as that used by St. Paul: " My little children, of whom I travail in birth again until Christ be formed in you " [1]; here St. Paul obviously cannot refer to a historical Jesus, but to some forth-putting from the human soul which is to him the shaping of Christ therein. Again the same teacher declares that though he had known Christ after the flesh, yet from henceforth he would know him thus no more [2]; obviously implying that while he recognized the Christ of the flesh—Jesus—there was a higher view to which he had attained which threw into the shade the historical Christ. This is the view which many are seeking in our own days, and—faced by the facts of Comparative Religion, puzzled by the contradictions of the Gospels, confused by problems they cannot solve so long as they are tied down to the mere surface meanings of their Scripture—they cry despairingly that the letter killeth while the spirit giveth life, and seek to trace some deep and wide significance in a story which is as old as the religions of the world, and has always served as the very centre and life of every religion in which it has reappeared. These struggling thinkers, too unrelated and indefinite to be spoken of as forming a school, seem to stretch out a hand on one side to those who think that all is legend, asking them to accept a historical basis; on the other side they say to their fellow Christians that

[1] Gal., iv, 19.
[2] II. Cor., v, 16.

there is growing danger lest, in calling to a literal and unique meaning, which cannot be defended before the increasing knowledge of the day, the spiritual meaning should be entirely lost. There is a danger of losing " the story of the Christ," with that thought of the Christ which has been the support and inspiration of millions of noble lives in East and West, though the Christ be called by other names and worshipped under other forms; a danger lest the pearl of great price should escape from our hold, and man be left the poorer for evermore.

What is needed, in order that this danger may be averted, is to disentangle the different threads in the story of the Christ, and to lay them side by side—the thread of history, the thread of legend, the thread of mysticism. These have been intertwined into a single strand, to the great loss of the thoughtful, and in disentangling them we shall find that the story becomes more, not less, valuable as knowledge is added to it, and that here, as in all that is basically of the truth, the brighter the light thrown upon it the greater the beauty that is revealed.

We will study first the historical Christ; secondly, the mythic Christ; thirdly, the mystic Christ. And we shall find that elements drawn from all these make up the Jesus Christ of the Churches. They all enter into the composition of the grandiose and pathetic Figure which dominates the thoughts and the emotions of Christendom, the Man of Sorrows, the Saviour, the Lover and Lord of Men.

THE HISTORICAL CHRIST
OR JESUS THE HEALER AND TEACHER

The thread of the life-story of Jesus is one which may be disentangled from those with which it is intertwined without any great difficulty. We may fairly here aid our study by reference to those records of the past which experts can reverify for themselves, and from which certain details regarding the Hebrew Teacher have been given to the world by H. P. Blavatsky and by others who are experts in occult investigation. Now in the minds of many there is apt to arise a challenge when this word " expert " is used in connection with occultism. Yet it only means a person who by special study, by special training, has accumulated a special kind of knowledge, and has developed powers that enable him to give an opinion founded on his own individual knowledge of the subject with which he is dealing. We may fairly call a man an expert in occultism who has first mastered intellectually certain fundamental theories of the constitution of man and the universe, and secondly has developed within himself the powers that are latent in everyone— and are capable of being developed by those who give themselves to appropriate studies—capacities which enable him to examine for himself the more obscure processes of nature. As a man may be born with a mathematical faculty, and by training that faculty year after year may immensely increase his mathematical capacity, so may a man be born with certain faculties

7

within him, faculties belonging to the Soul, which he can develop by training and by discipline. When, having developed those faculties, he applies them to the study of the invisible world, such a man becomes an expert in Occult Science, and such a man can at his will re-verify the records to which I have referred. Such re-verification is as much out of the reach of the ordinary person as a mathematical book written in the symbols of the higher mathematics is out of the reach of those who are untrained in mathematical science. There is nothing exclusive in the knowledge save as every science is exclusive; those who are born with a faculty, and train the faculty, can master its appropriate science, while those who start in life without any faculty, or those who do not develop it if they have it, must be content to remain in ignorance. These are the rules everywhere of the obtaining of knowledge, in Occultism as in every other science.

The occult records partly endorse the story told in the Gospels, and partly do not endorse it; they show us the life, and thus enable us to disentangle it from the myths which are intertwined therewith.

The child whose Jewish name has been turned into that of Jesus was born in Palestine B.C. 105, during the consulate of Publius Rutilius Rufus and Gnæus Mallius Maximus. His parents were well-born though poor, and he was educated in a knowledge of the Hebrew Scriptures. His fervent devotion and a gravity beyond his years led his parents to dedicate him to the religious and ascetic life, and soon after a visit to Jerusalem, in which the extraordinary intelligence and eagerness for knowledge of the youth were shown in his seeking of the doctors in the Temple, he was sent to be trained in an Essene community in the southern Judæan desert. When he had reached the age of nineteen he went on to the Essene monastery near Mount Serbal, a monastery which was much visited by learned men travelling from Persia and India to Egypt, and where a magnificent library of occult works—many of them Indian of the Trans-Himālayan regions—had been established. From this seat of mystic learning he proceeded later to Egypt. He had been fully instructed in the secret teachings which were the real fount of life among the Essenes, and was initiated in Egypt as a disciple of that one sublime Lodge from which every great religion has its Founder. For Egypt has remained one of the world-centres of the true Mysteries, whereof all semi-public Mysteries are the faint and far-off reflections. The mysteries spoken of in history as Egyptian were the shadows of the true things " in the Mount," and there the young Hebrew received the solemn consecration which prepared him for the royal priesthood he was later to attain. So superhumanly pure and so full of devotion was he, that in his gracious manhood he stood out pre-eminently from the severe and somewhat fanatical ascetics among whom he had been trained, shedding on the stern Jews around him the fragrance of a gentle and tender wisdom, as a rose-tree strangely planted in a desert would shed its sweetness on the barrenness around. The fair and stately grace of his white purity was round him as a radiant moonlit halo, and his words, though few, were ever sweet and loving, winning even the most harsh to a temporary gentleness, and the most rigid to a passing softness. Thus he lived through nine-and-twenty years of mortal life, growing from grace to grace.

This superhuman purity and devotion fitted the man Jesus, the disciple, to become the temple of a loftier Power, of a mighty, indwelling Presence. The time had come for one of those Divine manifestations which from age to age are made for the helping of humanity, when a new impulse is needed to quicken the spiritual evolution of mankind, when a new civilization is about to dawn. The world of the West was then in the womb of time, ready for the birth, and the Teutonic sub-race was to catch the sceptre of empire falling from the failing hands of Rome. Ere it started on its journey a World-Saviour must appear, to stand in blessing beside the cradle of the infant Hercules.

A mighty " Son of God " was to take flesh upon earth, a supreme Teacher, " full of grace and truth " [1] —One in whom the Divine Wisdom abode in fullest measure, who was verily " the Word " incarnate, Light and Life in outpouring richness, a very Fountain of the Waters of Life. Lord of Compassion and of Wisdom, such was His name—and from His dwelling in the Secret Places He came forth into the world of men.

For Him was needed an earthly tabernacle, a human form, the body of a man, and who so fit to yield his

[1] St. John, i, 14.

body in glad and willing service to One before whom Angels and men bow down in lowliest reverence, as this Hebrew of the Hebrews, this purest and noblest of " the Perfect," whose spotless body and stainless mind offered the best that humanity could bring? The man Jesus yielded himself a willing sacrifice, " offered himself without spot " to the Lord of Love, who took unto Himself that pure form as tabernacle, and dwelt therein for three years of mortal life.

This epoch is marked in the traditions embodied in the Gospels as that of the Baptism of Jesus, when the Spirit was seen " descending from heaven like a dove, and it abode upon him," [1] and a celestial voice proclaimed Him as the beloved Son, to whom men should give ear. Truly was He the beloved Son in whom the Father was well-pleased,[2] and from that time forward " Jesus began to preach," [3] and was that wondrous mystery, " God manifest in the flesh " [4]—not unique in that He was God, for: " Is it not written in your law, I said, Ye are Gods? If he called them Gods, unto whom the word of God came, and the scripture cannot be broken; say ye of Him, whom the Father hath sanctified and sent into the world, Thou blasphemest; because I said, I am the Son of God? " [5] Truly all men are Gods, in respect to the Spirit within them, but not in all is the

[1] St. John, i, 32.
[2] St. Matt., iii, 17.
[3] *Ibid.*, iv, 17.
[4] I. Tim., iii, 16.
[5] St. John, x, 34-36

God-head manifested, as in that well-beloved Son of the Most High.

To that manifested Presence the name of " the Christ " may rightly be given, and it was He who lived and moved in the form of the man Jesus over the hills and plains of Palestine, teaching, healing diseases, and gathering round Him as disciples a few of the more advanced souls. The rare charm of His royal love, outpouring from Him as rays from a sun, drew round Him the suffering, the weary, and the oppressed, and the subtly tender magic of His gentle wisdom purified, ennobled, and sweetened the lives that came into contact with His own. By parable and luminous imagery He taught the uninstructed crowds who pressed around Him, and, using the powers of the free Spirit, He healed many a disease by word or touch, reinforcing the magnetic energies belonging to His pure body with the compelling force of His inner life. Rejected by his Essene brethren among whom He first laboured—whose arguments against His purposed life of loving labour are summarized in the story of the temptation—because he carried to the people the spiritual wisdom that they regarded as their proudest and most secret treasure, and because His all-embracing love drew within its circle the outcast and the degraded—ever loving in the lowest as in the highest, the Divine Self—He saw gathering round Him all too quickly the dark clouds of hatred and suspicion. The teachers and rulers of His nation soon came to eye Him with jealousy and anger; His spirituality was a constant reproach to their materialism, His power a constant, though silent, exposure of their weakness. Three years had scarcely passed since His baptism when the gathering storm outbroke, and the human body of Jesus paid the penalty for enshrining the glorious Presence of a Teacher more than man.

The little band of chosen disciples whom He had selected as respositories of His teachings were thus deprived of their Master's physical presence ere they had assimilated His instructions, but they were souls of high and advanced type, ready to learn the Wisdom, and fit to hand it on to lesser men. Most receptive of all was that " disciple whom Jesus loved," young, eager and fervid, profoundly devoted to his Master, and sharing His spirit of all-embracing love. He represented, through the century that followed the physical departure of the Christ, the spirit of mystic devotion that sought the ecstasies, the vision of and the union with the Divine, while the later great Apostle, St. Paul, represented the wisdom side of the Mysteries.

The Master did not forget His promise to come to them after the world had lost sight of Him,[1] and for something over fifty years He visited them in His subtle spiritual body, continuing the teachings He had begun while with them, and training them in a knowledge of occult truths. They lived together, for the most part, in a retired spot on the outskirts of Judæa, attracting no attention among the many apparently similar communities of the time, studying the profound truths He taught them and acquiring " the gifts of the Spirit."

[1] St. John, xiv, 18, 19.

These inner instructions, commenced during His physical life among them and carried on after He had left the body, formed the basis of the " Mysteries of Jesus," which we have seen in early Church History, and gave the inner life which was the nucleus round which gathered the heterogeneous materials which formed ecclesiastical Christianity.

In the remarkable fragment called the *Pistis Sophia*, we have a document of the greatest interest bearing on the hidden teaching, written by the famous Valentinus. In this it is said that during the eleven years immediately after His death Jesus instructed His disciples so far as " the regions of the first statutes only, and up to the regions of the first mystery, the mystery within the veil." [1]   They had not so far learned the distribution of the angelic orders, of part whereof Ignatius speaks.[2] Then Jesus, being " in the Mount " with His disciples, and having received His mystic Vesture, the knowledge of all the regions and the Words of Power which unlocked them, taught His disciples further, promising: " I will perfect you in every perfection, from the mysteries of the interior to the mysteries of the exterior: I will fill you with the Spirit, so that ye shall be called spiritual, perfect in all perfections." [3]   And He taught them of Sophia, the Wisdom, and of her fall into matter in her attempt to rise unto the Highest, and of her cries to the Light in which she had trusted, and of the sending

[1] Valentinus, Trans., by G. R. S. Mead, *Pistis Sophia*, bk. i, 1.
[2] *Ante*, p. 52.
[3] *Ibid.*, 51.

of Jesus to redeem her from chaos, and of her crowning with His light, and leading forth from bondage. And He told them further of the highest Mystery, the ineffable, the simplest and clearest of all, though the highest, to be known by him alone who utterly renounced the world [1] ; by that knowledge men became Christs, for such " men are myself, and I am these men," for Christ is that highest Mystery,[2] knowing that men are "transformed into pure light and are brought into the light." [3]   And He performed for them the great ceremony of Initiation, the baptism " which leadeth to the region of truth and into the region of light," and bade them celebrate it for others who were worthy: " But hide ye this mystery, give it not unto every man, but unto him (only) who shall do all things which I have said unto you in my commandments." [4]

Thereafter, being fully instructed, the apostles went forth to preach, ever aided by their Master.

Moreover these same disciples and their earliest colleagues wrote down from memory all the public sayings and parables of the Master that they had heard, and collected with great eagerness any reports they could find, writing down these also, and circulating them all among those who gradually attached themselves to their small community. Various collections were made, any member writing down what he himself remembered, and

[1] *Ibid*, bk. ii, 218.
[2] *Ibid.*, 230.
[3] *Ibid.*, 357.
[4] *Ibid.*, 377.

adding selections from the accounts of others. The inner teachings, given by the Christ to His chosen ones, were not written down, but were taught orally to those deemed worthy to receive them, to students who formed small communities for leading a retired life, and remained in touch with the central body.

The historical Christ, then, is a glorious Being belonging to the great spiritual hiearchy that guides the spiritual evolution of humanity, who used for some three years the human body of the disciple Jesus; who spent the last of these three years in public teaching throughout Judæa and Samaria; who was a healer of diseases and performed other remarkable occult works; who gathered round Him a small band of disciples whom He instructed in the deeper truths of the spiritual life; who drew men to Him by the singular love and tenderness and the rich wisdom that breathed from His Person; and who was finally put to death for blasphemy, for teaching the inherent Divinity of Himself and of all men. He came to give a new impulse of spiritual life to the world; to re-issue the inner teachings affecting spiritual life; to mark out again the narrow ancient way; to proclaim the existence of the " Kingdom of Heaven," of the Initiation which admits to that knowledge of God which is eternal life; and to admit a few to that Kingdom who should be able to teach others. Round this glorious Figure gathered the myths which united Him to the long array of His predecessors, the myths telling in allegory the story of all such lives, as they symbolize the work of the Logos in the Kosmos and the higher evolution of the individual human soul.

But it must not be supposed that the work of the Christ for His followers was over after He had established the Mysteries, or was confined to rare appearances therein. That Mighty One who had used the body of Jesus as His vehicle, and whose guardian care extends over the whole spiritual evolution of the fifth root race of humanity, gave into the strong hands of the holy disciple who had surrendered to Him His body the care of the infant Church. Perfecting His human evolution, Jesus became one of the Masters of Wisdom, and took Christianity under His special charge, ever seeking to guide it to the right lines, to protect, to guard and nourish it. He was the Hierophant in the Christian Mysteries, the direct Teacher of the Initiates. His the inspiration that kept alight the Gnosis in the Church, until the superincumbent mass of ignorance became so great that even His breath could not fan the flame sufficiently to prevent its extinguishment. His the patient labour which strengthened soul after soul to endure through the darkness, and cherish within itself the spark of mystic longing, the thirst to find the Hidden God. His the steady inpouring of truth into every brain ready to receive it, so that hand stretched out to hand across the centuries and passed on the torch of knowledge which thus was never extinguished. His the Form which stood beside the rack and in the flames of the burning pile, cheering His confessors and His martyrs, soothing the anguish of their pains, and filling their hearts with

His peace. His the impulse which spoke in the thunder of Savonarola, which guided the calm wisdom of Erasmus, which inspired the deep ethics of the God-intoxicated Spinoza. His the energy which impelled Roger Bacon, Galileo and Paracelsus in their searchings into nature. His the beauty that allured Fra Angelica and Raphael and Leonardo da Vinci, that inspired the genius of Michael Angelo, that shone before the eyes of Murillo, and that gave the power that raised the marvels of the world, the Duomo of Milan, the San Marco of Venice, the Cathedral of Florence. His the melody that breathed in the masses of Mozart, the sonatas of Beethoven, the oratorios of Handel, the fugues of Bach, the austere splendour of Brahms. His the Presence that cheered the solitary mystics, the hunted occultists, the patient seekers after truth. By persuasion and by menace, by the eloquence of a St. Francis and by the gibes of a Voltaire, by the sweet submission of a Thomas à Kempis, and the rough virility of a Luther, He sought to instruct and awaken, to win into holiness or to scourge from evil. Through the long centuries He has striven and laboured, and with all the mighty burden of the Churches to carry, He has never left uncared for or unsolaced one human heart that cried to Him for help. And now He is striving to turn to the benefit of Christendom part of the great flood of the Wisdom poured out for the refreshing of the world, and He is seeking through the Churches for some who have ears to hear the Wisdom, and who will answer to His appeal for messengers to carry it to His flock: " Here am I; send me."

CHAPTER V

THE MYTHIC CHRIST

WE have already seen the use that is made of comparative mythology against religion, and some of its most destructive attacks have been levelled against the Christ. His birth of a Virgin at " Christmas," the slaughter of the Innocents, His wonder-working and His teachings, His crucifixion, resurrection and ascension—all these events in the story of His life are pointed to in the stories of other lives, and His historical existence is challenged on the strength of these identities. So far as the wonder-working and the teachings are concerned, we may briefly dismiss these first with the acknowledgement that most great Teachers have wrought works which, on the physical plane, appear as miracles in the sight of their contemporaries, but are known by occultists to be done by the exercise of powers possessed by all Initiates above a certain grade. The teachings He gave may also be acknowledged to be non-original; but where the student of comparative mythology thinks that he has proved that none is divinely inspired, when he shows that similar moral teachings fell from the lips of Manu, from the lips of the Buddha, from the lips of Jesus, the occultist says that certainly Jesus must have repeated the teachings of His predecessors, since He was a messenger from the same Brotherhood.   The profound verities touching the divine and the human Spirit were as much truths twenty thousand years before Jesus was born in Palestine as after He was born; and to say that the world was left without such teaching, and that man was left in moral darkness from his beginnings to twenty centuries ago, is to say that there was a humanity without a Teacher, children without a Father, human souls crying for light into a darkness that gave them no answer—a conception as blasphemous of God as it is desperate for man, a conception contradicted by the appearance of every Sage, by the mighty literature, by the noble lives, in the thousands of ages ere the Christ came forth.

Recognizing then in Jesus the great Master of the West, the leading Messenger of the Brotherhood of the western world, we must face the difficulty which has made havoc of this belief in the minds of many. Why are the festivals that commemorate events in the life of Jesus found in pre-Christian religions, and in them commemorate identical events in the lives of other Teachers?

Comparative mythology, which has drawn public attention to this question in modern times, may be said to be more than a century old, dating from the appearance of Dulaure's *Historie Abrégée de differens Cultes*, of Dupuis' *Origine de tous les Cultes*, of Moor's *Hindu Pantheon*, and of Godfrey Higgins' *Anacalypsis*. These works were followed by a shoal of others, growing more scientific and rigid in their collection and comparison of facts, until it has become impossible for any educated person to even challenge the identities and similarities existing in every direction. It is well known that in the first centuries " after Christ " these likenesses were on all hands admitted, and that modern comparative mythology is only repeating with great precision that which was universally recognized in the early Church. Justin Martyr, for instance, crowds his pages with references to the religions of his time, and if a modern assailant of Christianity would cite a number of cases in which Christian teachings are identical with those of elder religions, he can find no better guides than the apologists of the second century. They quote pagan teachings, stories and symbols, pleading that the very identity of the Christian with these should prevent the offhand rejection of the latter as in themselves incredible. A curious reason is, indeed, given for this identity, one that will scarcely find many adherents in modern days. Says Justin Martyr: " These who hand down the myths which the poets have made adduce no proof to the youths who learn them; and we proceed to demonstrate that they have been uttered by the influence of the wicked demons, to deceive and lead astray the human race. For having heard it proclaimed through the prophets that the Christ was to come, and that the ungodly among men were to be punished by fire, they put forward many to be called sons of Jupiter, under the impression that they would be able to produce in men the idea that the things which were said with regard to Christ were mere marvellous tales, like the things which were said by the poets." " And the devils, indeed, having heard this washing published by the prophet, instigated those who enter their temples, and are about to approach them with libations and burnt offerings, also to sprinkle themselves; and they cause them also to wash themselves entirely as they depart." " Which (the Lord's Supper) the wicked devils have imitated in the mysteries of Mithras, commanding the same thing to be done." [1] " For I myself, when I discovered the wicked disguise which the evil spirits had thrown around the divine doctrines of the Christians, to turn aside others from joining them, laughed." [2]

These identities were thus regarded as the work of devils, copies of the Christian originals, largely circulated in the pre-Christian world with the object of prejudicing the reception of the truth when it came. There is a certain difficulty in accepting the earlier statements as copies and the later as originals, but without disputing with Justin Martyr whether the copies preceded the original or the original the copies, we may be content to accept his testimony as to the existence of these identities between the faith flourishing in the Roman empire of his time and the new religion he was engaged in defending.

Tertullian speaks equally plainly, stating the objection made in his days also to Christianity, that " the nations who are strangers to all understanding of spiritual powers, ascribe to their idols the imbuing of waters with the self-same efficacy." " So they do," he answers quite frankly, " but these cheat themselves with waters

[1] Vol. II, Justin Martyr. *First Apology*, §§ liv, lxii and lxvi.
[2] Vol. II, Justin Martyr. *Second Apology*, § xiii.

that are widowed. For washing is the channel through which they are initiated into some sacred rites of some notorious Isis or Mithra; and the Gods themselves they honour by washings. . . . At the Apollinarian and Eleusinian games they are baptized; and they presume that the effect of their doing that is the regeneration and the remission of the penalties due to their perjuries. Which fact, being acknowledged, we recognize here also the zeal of the devil rivalling the things of God, while we find him too practising baptism in his subjects." [1]

To solve the difficulty of these identities we must study the Mythic Christ, the Christ of the solar myths or legends, these myths being the pictorial forms in which certain profound truths were given to the world.

Now a " myth " is by no means what most people imagine it to be—a mere fanciful story erected on a basis of fact, or even altogether apart from fact. A myth is far truer than a history, for a history only gives a story of the shadows, whereas a myth gives a story of the substances that cast the shadows. As above so below; and *first* above and *then* below. There are certain great principles according to which our system is built; there are certain laws by which these principles are worked out in detail; there are certain Beings who embody the principles and whose activities are the laws; there are hosts of inferior beings who act as vehicles for these activities, as agents, as instruments; there are the Egos of men intermingled with all these, performing their share of the great kosmic drama. These multifarious

[1] Vol. VII. Tertullian, *On Baptism*, ch. v.

8

workers in the invisible worlds cast their shadows on physical matter, and these shadows are " things "— the bodies, the objects, that make up the physical universe. These shadows give but a poor idea of the objects that cast them, just as what we call shadows down here give but a poor idea of the objects that cast them; they are mere outlines, with blank darkness in lieu of details, and have only length and breadth, no depth.

History is an account, very imperfect and often distorted, of the dance of these shadows in the shadow-world of physical matter. Anyone who has seen a clever shadow-play, and has compared what goes on behind the screen on which the shadows are cast with the movements of the shadows on the screen, may have a vivid idea of the illusory nature of the shadow-actions, and may draw therefrom several not misleading analogies.[1]

Myth is an account of the movements of those who cast the shadows; and the language in which the account is given is what is called the language of symbols. Just as here we have words which stand for things—as the word " table " is a symbol for a recognized article of a certain kind—so do symbols stand for objects on higher planes. They are a pictorial alphabet, used by all myth-writers and each has its recognized meaning. A symbol is used to signify a certain object just as words are used down here to distinguish one thing from

---

[1] The student might read Plato's account of the " Cave " and its inhabitants, remembering that Plato was an Initiate. *Republic*, bk. vii.

another, and so a knowledge of symbol is necessary for the reading of a myth. For the original tellers of great myths are ever Initiates, who are accustomed to use the symbolic language, and who, of course, use symbols in their fixed and accepted meanings.

A symbol has a chief meaning, and then various subsidiary meanings related to that chief meaning. For instance, the Sun is the symbol of the Logos; that is its chief or primary significance. But it stands also for an incarnation of the Logos, or for any of the great Messengers who represent Him for the time, as an ambassador represents his King. High Initiates who are sent on special missions to incarnate among men and live with them for a time as Rulers or Teachers, would be designated by the symbol of the Sun; for though it is not their symbol in an individual sense, it is theirs in virtue of their office.

All those who are signified by this symbol have certain characteristics, pass through certain situations, perform certain activities, during their lives on earth. The Sun is the physical shadow, or body, as it is called, of the Logos; hence its yearly course in nature reflects His activity, in the partial way in which a shadow represents the activity of the object that casts it. The Logos, " the Son of God," descending into matter, has as shadow the annual course of the Sun, and the Sun-Myth tells it. Hence, again, an incarnation of the Logos, or one of His high ambassadors, will also represent that activity, shadow-like, in His body as a man. Thus will necessarily arise identities in the life-histories of those ambassadors. In fact, the absence of such identities would at once point out that the person concerned was not a full ambassador, and that his mission was of a lower order.

The Solar Myth, then, is a story which primarily representing the activity of the Logos, or Word, in the kosmos, secondarily embodies the life of one who is an incarnation of the Logos, or is one of His ambassadors. The Hero of the myth is usually represented as a God, or Demi-God, and his life, as will be understood by what has been said above, must be outlined by the course of the Sun, as the shadow of the Logos. The part of the course lived out during the human life is that which falls between the winter solstice and the reaching of the zenith in summer. The Hero is born at the winter solstice, dies at the spring equinox, and, conquering death, rises into mid-heaven.

The following remarks are interesting in this connection, though looking at myth in a more general way, as an allegory, picturing inner truths: " Alfred de Vigny has said that legend is frequently more true than history, because legend recounts not acts which are often incomplete and abortive, but the genius itself of great men and great nations. It is pre-eminently to the Gospel that this beautiful thought is applicable, for the Gospel is not merely the narration of what has been; it is the sublime narration of what is and what always will be. Ever will the Saviour of the world be adored by the kings of intelligence, represented by the Magi; ever will He multiply the eucharistic bread, to nourish and comfort our souls; ever, when we invoke Him in the night and the tempest, will He come to us walking on the waters, ever will He stretch forth His hand and make us pass over the crests of the billows; ever will He cure our distempers and give back light to our eyes: ever will He appear to His faithful, luminous and trans-figured upon Tabor, interpreting the law of Moses and moderating the zeal of Elias." [1]

We shall find that myths are very closely related to the Mysteries, for part of the Mysteries consisted in showing living pictures of the occurrences in the higher worlds that became embodied in myths. In fact in the Pseudo-Mysteries, mutilated fragments of the living pictures of the true Mysteries were represented by actors who acted out a drama, and many secondary myths are these dramas put into words.

The broad outlines of the story of the Sun-God are very clear, the eventful life of the Sun-God being spanned within the first six months of the solar year, the other six being employed in the general protecting and preserving. He is always born at the winter sols-tice, after the shortest day in the year, at the midnight of the 24th of December, when the sign Virgo is rising above the horizon; born as this sign is rising, he is born always of a virgin, and she remains a virgin after she has given birth to her Sun-Child, as the celestial Virgo remains unchanged and unsullied when the Sun comes forth from her in the heavens. Weak, feeble as an in-fant is he, born, when the days are shortest and the

[1] Éliphas Lévi. *The Mysteries of Magic*, p. 48.

nights are longest—we are on the north of the equatorial line—surrounded with perils in his infancy, and the reign of the darkness far longer than his in his early days. But he lives through all the threatening dangers, and the day lengthens towards the spring equinox, till the time comes for the crossing over, the crucifixion, the date varying with each year. The Sun-God is sometimes found sculptured within the circle of the horizon, with the head and feet touching the circle at north and south, and the outstretched hands at east and west—" He was crucified." After this he rises triumphantly and ascends into heaven, and ripens the corn and the grape, giving his very life to them to make their substance and through them to his worshippers. The God who is born at the dawning of December 25th is ever crucified at the spring equinox, and ever gives his life as food to his worshippers—these are among the most salient marks of the Sun-God. The fixity of the birth-date and the variableness of the death-date are full of significance, when we remember that the one is a fixed and the other a variable solar position. " Easter " is a movable event, calculated by the relative positions of sun and moon, an impossible way of fixing year by year the anniversary of a historical event, but a very natural and indeed inevitable way of calculating a solar festival. These changing dates do not point to the history of a man, but to the Hero of a solar myth.

These events are reproduced in the lives of the various Solar Gods, and antiquity teems with illustrations of them. Isis of Egypt like Mary of Bethlehem was our Inmaculate Lady, Star of the Sea, Queen of Heaven, Mother of God. We see her in pictures standing on the crescent moon, star-crowned; she nurses her child Horus, and the cross appears on the back of the seat in which he sits on his mother's knee. The Virgo of the Zodiac is represented in ancient drawings as a woman suckling a child—the type of all future Madonnas with their divine Babes, showing the origin of the symbol. Devaki is likewise figured with the divine Krishna in her arms, as is Mylitta, or Istar, of Babylon, also with the recurrent crown of stars, and with her child Tammuz on her knee. Mercury and Aesculapius, Bacchus and Hercules, Perseus and the Dioscuri, Mithras and Zarathustra, were all of divine and human birth.

The relation of the winter solstice to Jesus is also significant. The birth of Mithras was celebrated in the winter solstice with great rejoicings, and Horus was also then born: "His birth is one of the greatest mysteries of the (Egyptian) religion. Pictures representing it appeared on the walls of temples. . . . He was the child of Deity. At Christmas time, or that answering to our festival, his image was brought out of the sanctuary with peculiar ceremonies, as the image of the infant Bambino is still brought out and exhibited at Rome." [1]

On the fixing of the 25th December as the birthday of Jesus, Williamson has the following: "All Christians know that the 25th December is *now* the recognized festival of the birth of Jesus, but few are aware that this

[1] Bonwick. *Egyptian Belief*, p. 157. Quoted in Williamson's *Great Law*, p. 26.

has not always been so. There have been, it is said, one hundred and thirty-six different dates fixed on by different Christian sects. Lightfoot gives it as 15th September, others as in February or August. Epiphanius mentions two sects, one celebrating it in June, the other in July. The matter was finally settled by Pope Julius I, in 337 A.D., and St. Chrysostom, writing in 390, says: " On this day (*i.e.*, 25th December also the birth of Christ was lately fixed at Rome, in order that while the heathen were busy with their ceremonies (the Brumalia, in honour of Bacchus) the Christians might perform their rites undisturbed." Gibbon in his *Decline and Fall of the Roman Empire*, writes: " The (Christian) Romans, as ignorant as their brethren of the real date of his (Christ's) birth, fixed the solemn festival to the 25th December, the Brumalia or winter solstice, when the Pagans annually celebrated the birth of the Sun." King in *Gnostics and Their Remains*, also says: " The ancient festival held on the 25th December in honour of the birthday of the Invincible One,[1] and celebrated by the great games at the Circus, was afterwards transferred to the commemoration of the birth of Christ, the precise date of which many of the Fathers confess was then unknown "; while at the present day Canon Farrar writes that " all attempts to discover the month and day of the nativity are useless. No data whatever exist to enable us to determine them with even approximate accuracy." From the foregoing it is

[1] The festival " Natalis Solis Invicti," the birthday of the Invincible Sun.

apparent that the great festival of the winter solstice has been celebrated during past ages, and in widely separated lands, in honour of the birth of a God, who is almost invariably alluded to as a ' Saviour,' and whose mother is referred to as a pure virgin. The striking resemblances, too, which have been instanced not only in the birth but in the life of so many of these Saviour-Gods are far too numerous to be accounted for by any mere coincidence." [1]

In the case of the Lord Buddha we may see how a myth attaches itself to a historical personage. The story of His life is well known, and in the current Indian accounts the birth-story is simple and human. But in the Chinese account He is born of a virgin, Māyādevi, the archaic myth finding in Him a new Hero.

Williamson also tells us that fires were and are lighted on the 25th December on the hills among Keltic peoples, and these are still known among the Irish and the Scotch Highlanders as Bheil or Baaltinne, the fires thus bearing the name of Bel, Bal, or Baal, their ancient Deity, the Sun-God, though now lighted in honour of Christ. [2]

Rightly considered, the Christmas festival should take on new elements of rejoicing and of sacredness, when the lovers of Christ see in it the repetition of an ancient solemnity, see it stretching all the world over, and far,

[1] Williamson. *The Great Law*, pp. 40-42. Those who wish to study this matter as one of Comparative Religion cannot do better than read *The Great Law*, whose author is a profoundly religious man and a Christian.

[2] *Ibid.*, pp. 36, 37.

far back into dim antiquity; so that the Christmas bells are ringing throughout human history, and sound musically out of the far-off night of time. Not in exclusive possession, but in universal acceptance, is found the hall-mark of truth.

The death-date, as said above, is not a fixed one, like the birth-date. The date of the death is calculated by the relative positions of Sun and Moon at the spring equinox, varying with each year, and the death-date of each Solar Hero is found to be celebrated in this connection. The animal adopted as the symbol of the Hero is the sign of the Zodiac in which the Sun is at the vernal equinox of his age, and this varies with the precession of the equinoxes. Oannes of Assyria had the sign of Pisces, the Fish, and is thus figured. Mithra is in Taurus, and, therefore, rides on a Bull, and Osiris was worshipped as Osiris-Apis, or Serapis, the Bull. Merodach of Babylon was worshipped as a Bull, as was Astarte of Syria. When the Sun is in the sign of Aries, the Ram or Lamb, we have Osiris again as Ram, and so also Astarte and Jupiter Ammon, and it is this same animal that became the symbol of Jesus—the Lamb of God. The use of the Lamb as His symbol, often leaning on a cross, is common in the sculptures of the catacombs. On this Williamson says: " In the course of time the Lamb was represented on the cross, but it was not until the sixth synod of Constantinople, held about the year 680, that it was ordained that instead of the ancient symbol, the figure of *a man* fastened to a cross should be represented. This canon was confirmed by

Pope Adrian I." [1] The very ancient Pisces is also assigned to Jesus, and He is thus pictured in the catacombs.

The death and resurrection of the Solar Hero at or about the vernal equinox is as widespread as his birth at the winter solstice. Osiris was then slain by Typhon, and He is pictured on the circle of the horizon, with outstretched arms, as if crucified—a posture originally of benediction, not of suffering. The death of Tammuz was annually bewailed at the spring equinox in Babylonia and Syria, as were Adonis in Syria and Greece, and Attis in Phrygia, pictured " as a man fastened with a lamb at the foot." [2] Mithras' death was similarly celebrated in Persia, and that of Bacchus and Dionysius —one and the same—in Greece. In Mexico the same idea reappears, as usual accompanied with the cross.

In all these cases the mourning for the death is immediately followed by the rejoicing over the resurrection, and on this it is interesting to notice that the name of Easter has been traced to the virgin-mother of the slain Tammuz, Ishtar. [3]

It is interesting also to notice that the fast preceding the death at the vernal equinox,—the modern Lent—is found in Mexico, Egypt, Persia, Babylon, Assyria, Asia Minor, in some cases definitely for forty days. [4]

[1] *The Great Law*, p. 116.
[2] *Ibid.*, p. 58.
[3] *Ibid.*, p. 56.
[4] *Ibid.*, pp. 120-123.

In the Pseudo-Mysteries, the Sun-God story was dramatized, and in the ancient Mysteries it was lived by the Initiate, and hence the solar " myths " and the great facts of Initiation became interwoven together. Hence when the Master Christ became the Christ of the Mysteries, the legends of the older Heroes of those Mysteries gathered round Him, and the stories were again recited with the latest divine Teacher as the representative of the Logos in the Sun.   Then the festival of His nativity became the immemorial date when the Sun was born of the Virgin, when the midnight sky was filled with the rejoicing hosts of the celestials, and

Very early, very early, Christ was born.

As the great legend of the Sun gathered round Him, the sign of the Lamb became that of His crucifixion as the sign of the Virgin had become that of His birth. We have seen that the Bull was sacred to Mithras and the Fish to Oannes, and that the Lamb was sacred to Christ, and for the same reason; it was the sign of the spring equinox, at the period of history in which He crossed the great circle of the horizon, was " crucified in space ".

These Sun myths, ever recurring throughout the ages, with a different name for their Hero in each new recension, cannot pass unrecognized by the student, though they may naturally and rightly be ignored by the devotee; and when they are used as a weapon to mutilate or destroy the majestic figure of the Christ, they must be met, not by denying the facts, but by understanding the deeper meaning of the stories, the spiritual truths that the legends expressed under a veil.

Why have these legends mingled with the history of Jesus, and crystallized round Him, as a historical personage? These are really the stories not of a particular individual named Jesus but of the universal Christ: of a Man who symbolized a Divine Being, and who represented a fundamental truth in nature; a Man who filled a certain office and held a certain characteristic position towards humanity; standing towards humanity in a special relationship, renewed age after age, as generation succeeded generation, as race gave way to race. Hence He was, as are all such, the " Son of Man," a peculiar and distinctive title, the title of an office, not of an individual. The Christ of the Solar Myth was the Christ of the Mysteries, and we find the secret of the mythic in the mystic Christ.

CHAPTER VI

THE MYSTIC CHRIST

WE now approach that deeper side of the Christ story that gives it its real hold upon the hearts of men. We approach that perennial life which bubbles up from an unseen source, and so baptizes its representative with its lucent flood that human hearts cling round the Christ, and feel that they could almost more readily reject the apparent facts of history than deny that which they intuitively feel to be a vital, an essential truth of the higher life. We draw near the sacred portal of the Mysteries, and lift a corner of the veil that hides the sanctuary.

We have seen that, go back as far as we may into antiquity, we find everywhere recognized the existence of a hidden teaching, a secret doctrine, given under strict and exacting conditions to approved candidates by the Masters of Wisdom. Such candidates were initiated into "The Mysteries"—a name that covers in antiquity, as we have seen, all that was most spiritual in religion, all that was most profound in philosophy, all that was most valuable in science. Every great Teacher of antiquity passed through the Mysteries and the greatest were the Hierophants of the Mysteries; each who came forth into the world to speak of the invisible worlds had passed through the portal of Initiation and had learned the secret of the Holy Ones from Their own lips: each who came forth, came forth with the same story, and the solar myths are all versions of this story, identical in their essential features, varying only in their local colour.

This story is primarily that of the descent of the Logos into matter, and the Sun-God is aptly His symbol, since the Sun is His body, and He is often described as " He that dwelleth in the Sun ". In one aspect, the Christ of the Mysteries is the Logos descending into matter, and the great Sun-Myth is the popular teaching of this sublime truth. As in previous cases, the Divine Teacher, who brought the Ancient Wisdom and republished it in the world, was regarded as a special manifestation of the Logos, and the Jesus of the Churches was gradually draped with the stories which belonged to this great One; thus He became identified, in Christian nomenclature, with the Second Person in the Trinity, the Logos, or Word of God,[1] and the salient events recounted in the myth of the Sun-God became the salient events of the story of Jesus, regarded as the incarnate Deity, the " mythic Christ." As in the macrocosm, the kosmos, the Christ of the Mysteries represents the Logos, the Second Person in the Trinity, so in the microcosm, man, does He represent the second aspect of the Divine Spirit

[1] See on this the opening of the Johannine Gospel, i, 1-5. The name Logos, ascribed to the manifested God, shaping matter— " all things were made by Him "—is Platonic, and is hence directly derived from the Mysteries; ages before Plato, Vāk, Voice, derived from the same source, was used among Hindus.

in man—hence called in man "the Christ." [1] The second aspect of the Christ of the Mysteries is then the life of the Initiate, the life which is entered on at the first great Initiation, at which the Christ is born in man, and after which He develops in man. To make this quite intelligible, we must consider the conditions imposed on the candidate for Initiation, and the nature of the Spirit in man.

Only those could be recognized as candidates for Initiation who were already good as men count goodness, according to the strict measure of the law. Pure, holy, without defilement, clean from sin, living without transgression—such were some of the descriptive phrases used of them.[2] Intelligent also must they be, of well-developed and well-trained minds.[3] The evolution carried on in the world life after life, developing and mastering the powers of the mind, the emotions, and the moral sense, learning through exoteric religions, practising the discharge of duties, seeking to help and lift others—all this belongs to the ordinary life of an evolving man. When all this is done, the man has become "a good man," the Chrêstos of the Greeks, and this he must be ere he can become the Christos, the Anointed. Having accomplished the exoteric good life, he becomes a candidate for the esoteric life, and enters on the preparation for Initiation, which consists in the fulfilment of certain conditions.

[1] See *Ante*, pp. 82-83.
[2] See *Ante*, pp. 62-63.
[3] See *Ante*, pp. 56-57.

These conditions mark out the attributes he is to acquire, and while he is labouring to create these, he is sometimes said to be treading the Probationary Path, the Path which leads up to the " Strait Gate," beyond which is the " Narrow Way," or the " Path of Holiness," the " Way of the Cross." He is not expected to develop these attributes perfectly, but he must have made some progress in all of them, ere the Christ can be born in him. He must prepare a pure home for that Divine Child who is to develop within him.

The first of these attributes—they are all mental and moral—is *discrimination*; this means that the aspirant must begin to separate in his mind the eternal from the temporary, the real from the unreal, the true from the false, the heavenly from the earthly. " The things which are seen are temporal," says the Apostle: " but the things which are not seen are eternal." [1] Men are constantly living under the glamour of the seen, and are blinded by it to the unseen. The aspirant must learn to discriminate between them, so that what is unreal to the world may become real to him, and that which is real to the world may to him become unreal, for thus only is it possible to " walk by faith, not by sight." [2] And thus also must a man become one of those of whom the Apostle says that they " are of full age, even those who by reason of use have their senses exercised to discern both good and evil." [3] Next, this sense of unreality

[1] II. Cor., iv, 13.
[2] *Ibid.*, v, 7.
[3] Heb., v, 14.

must breed in him *disgust* with the unreal and the fleeting, the mere husks of life, unfit to satisfy hunger, save
the hunger of swine.[1] This stage is described in the
emphatic language of Jesus: "If any man come to me
and hate not his father, and mother, and wife, and
children, and brethren, and sisters, yea, and his own
life, also, he cannot be my disciple."[2] Truly a "hard
saying," and yet out of this hatred will spring a deeper,
truer, love, and the stage may not be escaped on the
way to the Strait Gate. Then the aspirant must learn
control of thoughts, and this will lead to *control of
actions*, the thought being, to the inner eye, the same
as the action: "Whosoever looketh on a woman to lust
after her, *hath committed adultery* with her already in
his heart."[3] He must acquire *endurance*, for they who
aspire to tread "the Way of the Cross" will have to
brave long and bitter sufferings, and they must be able
to endure, "as seeing him who is invisible."[4] He
must add to these *tolerance*, if he would be the child
of Him who "maketh his sun to rise on the evil, and
on the good, and sendeth rain on the just and on the
unjust,"[5] the disciple of Him who bade His apostles
not to forbid a man to use His name because he did not
follow with them.[6] Further, he must acquire the *faith*
to which nothing is impossible,[7] and the *balance* which
is described by the Apostle.[8] Lastly, he must seek

---

[1] St. Luke, xv, 16.　　　　[2] *Ibid.*, xiv, 26.
[3] St. Matt., v, 28.　　　　[4] Heb., xi, 27.
[5] St. Matt., v, 45.　　　　[6] Luke, ix, 49, 50.
[7] St. Matt., xvii, 20.　　　[8] II. Cor., vi, 8-10.

only " those things which are above," [1] and long to reach the beatitude of the vision of and union with God.[2] When a man has wrought these qualities into his character he is regarded as fit for Initiation, and the Guardians of the Mysteries will open for him the Strait Gate. Thus, but thus only, he becomes the prepared candidate.

Now, the Spirit in man is the gift of the Supreme God, and contains within itself the three aspects of the Divine Life—Intelligence, Love, Will—being the Image of God. As it evolves, it first develops the aspect of Intelligence, develops the intellect, and this evolution is effected in the ordinary life in the world. To have done this to a high point, accompanying it with moral development, brings the evolving man to the condition of the candidate. The second aspect of the Spirit is that of Love, and the evolution of that is the evolution of the Christ. In the true Mysteries this evolution is undergone—the disciple's life is the Mystery Drama, and the Great Initiations mark its stages. In the Mysteries performed on the physical plane these used to be dramatically represented, and the ceremonies followed in many respects " the pattern " ever shown forth " on the Mount," for they were the shadows in a deteriorating age of the mighty Realities in the spiritual world.

The Mystic Christ, then, is twofold—the Logos, the Second Person of the Trinity, descending into matter, and the Love, or second, aspect of the unfolding Divine Spirit in man. The one represents kosmic processes

[1] Col., iii, 1.   [2] St. Matt., v, 8; and St. John, xvii, 21.

carried on in the past and is the root of the Solar Myth: the other represents a process carried on in the individual, the concluding stage of his human evolution, and added many details in the Myth. Both of these have contributed to the Gospel story, and together form the Image of the " Mystic Christ."

Let us consider first the kosmic Christ, Deity becoming enveloped in matter, the becoming incarnate of the Logos, the clothing of God in " flesh."

When the matter which is to form our solar system is separated off from the infinite ocean of matter which fills space, the Third Person of the Trinity—the Holy Spirit—pours His Life into this matter to vivify it, that it may presently take form. It is then drawn together, and form is given to it by the life of the Logos, the Second Person of the Trinity, who sacrifices Himself by putting on the limitations of matter, becoming the " Heavenly Man," in whose Body all forms exist, of whose Body all forms are part. This was the kosmic story, dramatically shown in the Mysteries—in the true Mysteries seen as it occurred in space, in the physical plane Mysteries represented by magical or other means, and in some parts by actors.

These processes are very distinctly stated in the Bible: when the " Spirit of God moved upon the face of the waters " in the darkness that was " upon the face of the deep," [1] the great deep of matter showed no forms, it was void, inchoate. Form was given by the Logos, the Word, of whom it is written that " all things were made

[1] Gen., i, 2.

by him; and without him was not anything made that was made." [1] C. W. Leadbeater has well put it: "The result of this first great outpouring [the ' moving ' of the Spirit] is the quickening of that wonderful and glorious vitality which pervades all matter (inert though it may seem to our dim physical eyes), so that the atoms of the various planes develop, when electrified by it, all sorts of previously latent attractions and repulsions, and enter into combinations of all kinds." [2]

Only when this work of the Spirit has been done can the Logos, the kosmic Mystic Christ, take on Himself the clothing of matter, entering in very truth the Virgin's womb, the womb of Matter as yet virgin, unproductive. This matter had been vivified by the Holy Spirit, who, overshadowing the Virgin, poured into it His life, thus preparing it to receive the life of the Second Logos, who took this matter as the vehicle for His energies.   This is the becoming incarnate of the Christ, the taking flesh —" Thou did'st not despise the Virgin's womb."

In the Latin and English translations of the original Greek text of the Nicene Creed, the phrase which describes this phase of the descent has changed the prepositions and so changed the sense. The original ran: " and was incarnate *of* the Holy Ghost *and* the Virgin Mary," whereas the translation reads: " and was incarnate *by* the Holy Ghost *of* the Virgin Mary." [3]   The

[1] St. John, i, 3.

[2] *The Christian Creed*, p. 29.   This is a most valuable and fascinating little book, on the mystical meaning of the creeds.

[3] *Ibid.*, p. 42.

Christ " takes form not of the ' Virgin ' matter alone, but of matter which is already instinct and pulsating with the life of the Third Logos,[1] so that both the life and the matter surround Him as a vesture." [2]

This is the descent of the Logos into matter, described as the birth of the Christ of a Virgin, and this, in the Solar Myth, becomes the birth of the Sun-God as the sign Virgo rises.

Then come the early workings of the Logos in matter, aptly typified by the infancy of the myth. To all the feebleness of infancy His majestic powers bow themselves, letting but little play forth on the tender forms they ensoul. Matter imprisons, seems as though threatening to slay, its infant King, whose glory is veiled by the limitations He has assumed. Slowly He shapes it towards high ends, and lifts it into manhood, and then stretches Himself on the cross of matter that He may pour forth from that cross all the powers of His surrendered life. This is the Logos of whom Plato said that He was in the figure of a cross on the universe; this is the Heavenly Man, standing in space, with arms outstretched in blessing; this is the Christ crucified whose death on the cross of matter fills all matter with His life. Dead He seems and buried out of sight, but He rises again clothed in the very matter in which He seemed to perish, and carried up His body of now radiant matter into heaven, where it receives the downpouring life of the Father, and becomes the vehicle of

[1] A name of the Holy Ghost.

[2] *Ibid.*, p. 43.

man's immortal life. For it is the life of the Logos which forms the garment of the Soul in man, and He gives it that men may live through the ages and grow to the measure of His own stature. Truly are we clothed in Him, first materially and then spiritually. He sacrificed Himself to bring many sons into glory, and He is with us always, even to the end of the age.

The crucifixion of Christ, then, is part of the great kosmic sacrifice, and the allegorical representation of this in the physical Mysteries, and the sacred symbol of the crucified man in space, became materialized into an actual death by crucifixion, and a crucifix bearing a dying human form; then this story, now the story of a man, was attached to the Divine Teacher, Jesus, and became the story of His physical death, while the birth from a Virgin, the danger-encircled infancy, the resurrection and ascension, became also incidents in His human life. The mysteries disappeared, but their grandiose and graphic representations of the kosmic work of the Logos encircled and uplifted the beloved figure of the Teacher of Judæa, and the kosmic Christ of the Mysteries, with the lineaments of the Jesus of history, thus became the central Figure of the Christian Church.

But even this was not all; the last touch of fascination is added to the Christ-story by the fact that there is another Christ of the Mysteries, close and dear to the human heart—the Christ of the human Spirit, the Christ who is in every one of us, is born and lives, is crucified, rises from the dead, and ascends into heaven, in every suffering and triumphant " Son of Man."

The life-story of every initiate into the true, the heavenly Mysteries, is told in its salient features in the Gospel biography. For this reason, St. Paul speaks as we have seen [1] of the birth of the Christ in the disciple, and of His evolution and His full stature therein. Every man is a potential Christ, and the unfolding of the Christ-life in a man follows the outline of the Gospel story in its striking incidents, which we have seen to be universal, and not particular.

There are five great Initiations in the life of a Christ, each one marking a stage in the unfolding of the Life of Love. They are given now, as of old, and the last marks the final triumph of the Man who has developed into Divinity, who has transcended humanity, and has become a Saviour of the world.

Let us trace this life-story, ever newly repeated in spiritual experience, and see the Initiate living out the life of the Christ.

At the first great Initiation the Christ is born in the disciple; it is then that he realizes for the first time *in himself* the outpouring of the divine Love and experiences that marvellous change which makes him feel himself to be one with all that lives. This is the " Second Birth," and at that birth the heavenly ones rejoice, for he is born into " the kingdom of heaven," as one of the " little ones," as " a little child "—the names ever given to the new Initiates. Such is the meaning of the words of Jesus, that a man must become a

[1] *Ante*, p. 85.

little child to enter into the Kingdom.[1] It is significantly said in some of the early Christian writers that Jesus
was " born in a cave "—the " stable " of the gospel
narrative; the " Cave of Initiation " is a well-known
ancient phrase, and the Initiate is ever born therein;
over that cave " where the young child " is, burns the
" Star of Initiation," the Star that ever shines forth in
the East when a Child-Christ is born. Every such child
is surrounded by perils and menaces, strange dangers
that befall not other babes; for he is anointed with the
chrism of the second birth and the Dark Powers of the
unseen world ever seek his undoing. Despite all trials,
however, he grows into manhood, for the Christ once
born can never perish, the Christ once beginning to
develop can never fail in his evolution: his fair life expands and grows, ever-increasing in wisdom and in
spiritual stature, until the time comes for the second
great Initiation, the Baptism of the Christ by Water and
the Spirit, that gives him the powers necessary for the
Teacher, who is to go forth and labour in the world as
" the beloved Son."

Then there descends upon him in rich measure the
divine Spirit, and the glory of the unseen Father pours
down its pure radiance on him; but from that scene of
blessing is he led by the Spirit into the wilderness and
is once more exposed to the ordeal of fierce temptations.
For now the powers of the Spirit are unfolding themselves in him, and the Dark Ones strive to lure him from
his path by these very powers, bidding him use them

[1] St. Matt., xviii, 3.

for his own helping instead of resting on his Father in patient trust. In the swift, sudden transitions which test his strength and faith, the whisper of the embodied Tempter follows the voice of the Father, and the burning sands of the wilderness scorch the feet erstwhile bathed in the cool waters of the holy river. Conqueror over these temptations, he passes into the world of men to use for their helping the powers he would not put forth for his own needs, and he who would not turn one stone to bread for the stilling of his own cravings feeds "five thousand men, besides women and children," with a few loaves.

Into his life of ceaseless service comes another brief period of glory, when he ascends "a high mountain apart"—the sacred Mount of Initiation. There he is transfigured and there meets some of his great Forerunners, the Mighty Ones of old who trod where he now is treading. He passes thus the third great Initiation, and then the shadow of his coming Passion falls on him, and he steadfastly sets his face to go to Jerusalem —repelling the tempting words of one of his disciples— Jerusalem, where awaits him the baptism of the Holy Ghost and of Fire. After the Birth, the attack by Herod; after the Baptism, the temptation in the wilderness; after the Transfiguration, the setting forth towards the last stage of the Way of the Cross. Thus is triumph ever followed by ordeal, until the goal is reached.

Still grows the life of love, ever fuller and more perfect, the Son of Man shining forth more clearly as the Son of God, until the time draws near for his final battle, and the fourth great Initiation leads him in triumph into Jerusalem, into sight of Gethsemane and Calvary. He is now the Christ ready to be offered, ready for the sacrifice on the cross. He is now to face the bitter agony in the Garden, where even his chosen ones sleep while he wrestles with his mortal anguish, and for a moment prays that the cup may pass from his lips; but the strong will triumphs and he stretches out his hand to take and drink, and in his loneliness an angel comes to him and strengthens him, as angels are wont to do when they see a Son of Man bending beneath his load of agony. The drinking of the bitter cup of betrayal, of desertion, of denial, meets him as he goes forth, and alone amid his jeering foes he passes to his last fierce trial. Scourged by physical pain, pierced by cruel thorns of suspicion, stripped of his fair garments of purity in the eyes of the world, left in the hands of his foes, deserted apparently by God and man, he endures patiently all that befalls him, wistfully looking in his last extremity for aid. Left still to suffer, crucified, to die to the life of form, to surrender all life that belongs to the lower world, surrounded by triumphant foes who mock him, the last horror of great darkness envelopes him, and in the darkness he meets all the forces of evil; his inner vision is blinded, he finds himself alone, utterly alone, till the strong heart, sinking in despair, cries out to the Father who seems to have abandoned him, and the human soul faces, in uttermost loneliness, the crushing agony of apparent defeat. Yet, summoning all the strength of the " unconquerable spirit," the lower life is yielded up, its death is willingly embraced, the body of desire is abandoned, and the Initiate "descends into hell," that no region of the universe he is to help may remain untrodden by him, that none may be too outcast to be reached by his all-embracing love. And then springing upwards from the darkness, he sees the light once more, feels himself again as the Son, inseparable from the Father whose Son he is, rises to the life that knows no ending, radiant in the consciousness of death faced and overcome, strong to help to the uttermost every child of man, able to pour out his life into every struggling soul. Among his disciples he remains awhile to teach, unveiling to them the mysteries of the spiritual worlds, preparing them also to tread the path he has trodden, until, the earth-life over, he ascends to the Father, and, in the fifth great Initiation, becomes the Master triumphant, the link between God and man.

Such was the story lived through in the true Mysteries of old and new, and dramatically portrayed in symbols in the physical plane Mysteries, half veiled, half shown. Such is the Christ of the Mysteries in His dual aspect, Logos and man, kosmic and individual. Is it any wonder that this story, dimly felt, even when unknown, by the mystic, has woven itself into the heart, and served as an inspiration to all noble living? The Christ of the human heart is, for the most part, Jesus seen as the mystic human Christ, struggling, suffering, dying, finally triumphant, the Man in whom humanity in seen crucified and risen, whose victory is the promise of victory to every one who, like Him, is faithful through death and beyond—the Christ who can never be forgotten while He is born again and again in humanity, while the world needs Saviours, and Saviours give themselves for men.

CHAPTER VII

THE ATONEMENT

WE will now proceed to study certain aspects of the Christ Life, as they appear among the doctrines of Christianity. In the exoteric teachings they appear as attached only to the Person of the Christ; in the esoteric they are seen as belonging, indeed to Him since in their primary, their fullest and deepest meaning they form part of the activities of the Logos, but as being only secondarily reflected in the Christ, and therefore also in every Christ-Soul that treads the way of the Cross. Thus studied they will be seen to be profoundly true, while in their exoteric form they often bewilder the intelligence and jar the emotions.

Among these stands prominently forward the doctrine of the Atonement; not only has it been a point of bitter attack from those outside the pale of Christianity, but it has wrung many sensitive consciences within that pale. Some of the most deeply Christian thinkers have been tortured with doubts as to the teaching of the churches on this matter, and have striven to see, and to present it, in a way that softens or explains away the cruder notions based on an unintelligent reading of a few profoundly mystical texts. Nowhere, perhaps, more than in connection with these should the warning of St. Peter be borne in mind: " Our beloved brother Paul also, according to the wisdom given unto him, hath written unto you—as also in all his epistles—speaking in them of these things; in which are some things hard to be understood, which they that are unlearned and unstable wrest, as they do also the other scriptures, unto their own destruction." [1] For the texts that tell of the identity of the Christ with His brother-men have been wrested into a legal substitution of Himself for them, and have thus been used as an escape from the results of sin, instead of as an inspiration to righteousness.

The general teaching in the Early Church on the doctrine of the Atonement was that Christ, as the representative of humanity, faced and conquered Satan, the representative of Dark Powers, who held humanity in bondage, wrested his captive from him, and set him free. Slowly, as Christian teachers lost touch with spiritual truths, and they reflected their own increasing intolerance and harshness on the pure and loving Father of the teachings of the Christ, they represented Him as angry with man, and the Christ was made to save man from the wrath of God instead of from the bondage of evil. Then legal phrases intruded, still further materializing the once spiritual idea, and the " scheme of redemption " was forensically outlined. " The seal was set on the ' redemption scheme ' by Anselm in his great work, *Cur Deus Homo*, and the doctrine which had

[1] 2 St. Peter, iii, 15, 16.

been slowly growing into the theology of Christendom was thenceforward stamped with the signet of the Church. Roman Catholic and Protestant, at the time of the Reformation, alike believed in the vicarious and substitutionary character of the atonement wrought by Christ. There is no dispute between them on this point. I prefer to allow the Christian divines to speak for themselves as to the character of the atonement. . . . " Luther teaches that ' Christ did truly and effectually feel for all mankind the wrath of God, malediction, and death.' Flavel says that ' to wrath, to the wrath of an infinite God without mixture, to the very torments of hell, was Christ delivered and that, by the hand of his own father.' The Anglican homily preaches that ' sin did pluck God out of heaven to make him feel the horrors and pains of death,' and that man, being a firebrand of hell and a bondsman of the devil, ' was ransomed by the death of his only and well-beloved son '; the ' heat of his wrath,' ' his burning wrath,' could only be ' pacified ' by Jesus, ' so pleasant was the sacrifice and oblation of his son's death.' Edwards, being logical, saw that there was a gross injustice in sin being twice punished, and in the pains of hell, the penalty of sin, being twice inflicted, first on Jesus, the substitute of mankind, and then on the lost, a portion of mankind; so he, in common with most Calvinists, finds himself compelled to restrict the atonement to the elect, and declared that Christ bore the sins, not of the world, but of the chosen out of the world; he suffers ' not for the world, but for them whom thou hast given me.' But Edwards adheres firmly to the belief in substitution, and rejects the universal atonement for the very reason that ' to believe Christ died for all is the surest way of proving that he died for none in the sense Christians have hitherto believed.' He declares that ' Christ suffered the wrath of God for men's sins '; that ' God imposed his wrath due unto, and Christ underwent the pains of hell for, sin.' Owen regards Christ's sufferings as a ' full valuable compensation to the justice of God for all the sins ' of the elect, and says that he underwent ' that same punishment which . . . they themselves were bound to undergo.' " [1]

To show that these views were still authoritatively taught in the churches, I wrote further: " Stroud makes Christ drink ' the cup of the wrath of God.' Jenkyn says ' He suffered as one disowned and reprobated and forsaken of God.' Dwight considers that he endured God's ' hatred and contempt.' Bishop Jeune tells us that ' after man had done his worst, worse remained for Christ to bear. He had fallen into his father's hands.' Archbishop Thomson preaches that ' the clouds of God's wrath gathered thick over the whole human race: they discharged themselves on Jesus only.' He ' becomes a curse for us and a vessel of wrath.' Liddon echoes the same sentiment: ' The apostles teach that mankind are slaves, and that Christ on the cross is paying their ransom. Christ crucified is voluntarily devoted and accursed '; he even speaks of ' the precise amount of ignomity and pain needed for the redemption,' and

[1] A. Besant. *Essay on the Atonement.*

10

says that the ' divine victim ' paid more than was absolutely necessary." [1]

These are the views against which the learned and deeply religious Dr. McLeod Campbell wrote his well-known work, *On the Atonement*, a volume containing many true and beautiful thoughts; F. D. Maurice and many other Christian men have also striven to lift from Christianity the burden of a doctrine so destructive of all true ideas as to the relations between God and man.

None the less, as we look backwards over the effects produced by this doctrine, we find that belief in it, even in its legal—and to us crude exoteric—form, is connected with some of the very highest developments of Christian conduct, and that some of the noblest examples of Christian manhood and womanhood have drawn from it their strength, their inspiration, and their comfort. It would be unjust not to recognize this fact. And whenever we come upon a fact that seems to us startling and incongruous, we do well to pause upon that fact, and to endeavour to understand it. For this doctrine contained nothing more than is seen in it by its assailants inside and outside the churches, if it were in its true meaning as repellent to the conscience and the intellect as it is found to be by many thoughtful Christians, then it could not possibly have exercised over the minds and hearts of men a compelling fascination, nor could it have been the root of heroic self-surrenders, of touching and pathetic examples of self-sacrifice in the service of man. Something more there must be in it

[1] A. Besant. *Essay on the Atonement.*

than lies on the surface, some hidden kernel of life which has nourished those who have drawn from it their inspiration. In studying it as one of the Lesser Mysteries we shall find the hidden life which these noble ones have unconsciously absorbed, these souls which were so at one with that life that the form in which it was veiled could not repel them.

When we come to study it as one of the Lesser Mysteries, we shall feel that for its understanding some spiritual development is needed, some opening of the inner eyes. To grasp it requires that its spirit should be partly evolved in the life, and only those who know practically something of the meaning of self-surrender will be able to catch a glimpse of what is implied in the esoteric teaching on this doctrine, as the typical manifestation of the Law of Sacrifice. We can only understand it as applied to the Christ, when we see it as a special manifestation of the universal law, a reflection below of the Pattern above, showing us in a concrete human life what sacrifice means.

The Law of Sacrifice underlies our system and all systems, and on it all universes are builded. It lies at the root of evolution, and alone makes it intelligible. In the doctrine of the Atonement it takes a concrete form in connection with men who have reached a certain stage in spiritual development, the stage that enables them to realize their oneness with humanity, and to become, in very deed and truth, Saviours of men.

All the great religions of the world have declared that the universe begins by an act of sacrifice, and have incorporated the idea of sacrifice into their most solemn rites. In Hinduism, the dawn of manifestation is said to be by sacrifice,[1] mankind is emanated with sacrifice,[2] and it is Deity who sacrifices Himself;[3] the object of the sacrifice is manifestation; He cannot become manifest unless an act of sacrifice be performed, and inasmuch as nothing can be manifest until He manifests,[4] the act of sacrifice is called " the dawn " of creation.

In the Zoroastrian religion it was taught that in the Existence that is boundless, unknowable, unnameable, sacrifice was performed and manifest Deity appeared; Ahura-mazdâo was born of an act of sacrifice.[5]

In the Christian religion the same idea is indicated in the phrase; " the Lamb slain from the foundation of the world," [6] slain at the origin of things. These words can but refer to the important truth that there can be no founding of a world until the Deity has made an act of sacrifice. This act is explained as limiting Himself in order to become manifest. " The Law of Sacrifice might perhaps more truly be called The Law of Manifestation, or the Law of Love and of Life, for throughout the universe, from the highest to the lowest, it is the cause of manifestation and life." [7]

---

[1] *Brihadaranyakopanishat*, I, i, 1.

[2] *Bhagavad Gita*, iii, 10.

[3] *Brihadaranyakopanishat*, I, ii, 7.

[4] *Mundakopanishat*, II, ii, 10.

[5] Haug. *Essays on the Parsis*, pp. 12-14.

[6] Rev., xiii, 8.

[7] W. Williamson. *The Great Law*, p. 406.

" Now, if we study this physical world, as being the most available material, we find that all life in it, all growth, all progress, alike for units and for aggregates, depend on continual sacrifice and the endurance of pain. Mineral is sacrificed to vegetable, vegetable to animal, both to man, men to men, and all the higher forms again break up, and reinforce again with their separated constituents the lowest kingdom. It is a continual sequence of sacrifices from the lowest to the highest, and the very mark of progress is that the sacrifice from being involuntary and imposed becomes voluntary and self-chosen, and those who are recognized as greatest by man's intellect and loved most by man's heart are the supreme sufferers, those heroic souls who wrought, endured and died that the race might profit by their pain. If the world be the work of the Logos, and the law of the world's progress in the whole and the parts is sacrifice, then the Law of Sacrifice must point to something in the very nature of the Logos; it must have its root in the Divine Nature itself. A little further thought shows us that if there is to be a world, a universe at all, this can only be by the One Existence conditioning Itself and thus making manifestation possible, and that the very Logos is the Self-limited God; limited to become manifest; manifested to bring a universe into being; such self-limitation and manifestation can only be a supreme act of sacrifice, and what wonder that on every hand the world should show its birth-mark, and that the Law of Sacrifice should be the law of being, the law of the derived lives!

" Further, as it is an act of sacrifice in order that individuals may come into existence to share the Divine bliss, it is very truly a vicarious act—an act done for the sake of others; hence the fact already noted, that progress is marked by sacrifice becoming voluntary and self-chosen, and we realize that humanity reaches its perfection in the man who gives himself for men, and by his own suffering purchases for the race some lofty good.

" Here, in the highest regions, is the inmost verity of vicarious sacrifice, and however it may be degraded and distorted, this inner spiritual truth makes it indestructible, eternal, and the fount whence flows the spiritual energy which, in manifold forms and ways, redeems the world from evil and draws it home to God." [1]

When the Logos comes forth from " the bosom of the Father " in that " Day " when He is said to be " begotten," [2] the dawn of the Day of Creation, of Manifestation, when by Him God " made the worlds," [3] He by His own will limits Himself, making as it were a sphere enclosing the Divine Life, coming forth as a radiant orb of Deity, the Divine Substance, Spirit within and limitation, or Matter, without. This is the veil of matter which makes possible the birth of the Logos, Mary, the World-Mother, necessary for the manifestation in time of the Eternal, that Deity may manifest for the building of the worlds.

[1] A. Besant, *Nineteenth Century*, June, 1895. " The Atonement."

[2] Heb., i, 5.   [3] Heb., i, 2.

That circumscription, that self-limitation, is the act of sacrifice, a voluntary action done for love's sake, that other lives may be born from Him. Such a manifestation has been regarded as a death, for, in comparison with the unimaginable life of God in Himself, such circumscription in matter may truly be called death. It has been regarded, as we have seen, as a crucifixion in matter, and has been thus figured, the true origin of the symbol of the cross, whether in its so-called Greek form, wherein the vivifying of matter by the Holy Ghost is signified, or in its so-called Latin, whereby the Heavenly Man is figured, the supernal Christ. [1]

" In tracing the symbolism of the Latin cross, or rather of the crucifix, back into the night of time, the investigators had expected to find the figure disappear, leaving behind what they supposed to be the earlier cross-emblem. As a matter of fact exactly the reverse took place, and they were startled to find that eventually the cross drops away, leaving only the figure with uplifted arms. No longer is there any thought of pain or sorrow connected with that figure, though still it tells of sacrifice; rather is it now the symbol of the purest joy the world can hold—the joy of freely giving—for it typifies the Divine Man standing in space with arms upraised in blessing, casting abroad His gifts to all humanity, pouring forth freely of Himself in all directions, descending into that ' dense sea ' of matter, to be cribbed, cabined, and confined therein, in

[1] C. W. Leadbeater. *The Christian Creed*, pp. 54-56.

order that through that descent *we* may come into being." [1]

This sacrifice is perpetual, for in every form in this universe of infinite diversity this life is enfolded, and is its very heart, the " Heart of Silence " of the Egyptian ritual, the " Hidden God ". This sacrifice is the secret of evolution. The Divine Life, cabined within a form, ever presses outwards in order that the form may expand, but presses gently, lest the form should break ere yet it had reached its utmost limit of expansion. With infinite patience and tact and discretion, the divine One keeps up the constant pressure that expands, without losing a force that would disrupt. In every form, in mineral, in vegetable, in animal, in man, this expansive energy of the Logos is ceaselessly working. That is the evolutionary force, the lifting life within the forms, the rising energy that science glimpses, but knows not whence it comes. The botanist tells of an energy within the plant, that pulls ever upwards. Just as it is in plant life, so is it in other forms as well, making them more and more expressive of the life within them. When the limit of any form is reached, and it can grow no further, so that nothing more can be gained through it by the soul of it—that germ of Himself, which the Logos is brooding over—then He draws away His energy, and the form disintegrates—we call it death and decay. But the soul is with Him, and He shapes for it a new form, and the death of the form is the birth of the soul into fuller life. If we saw with the eyes

[1] C. W. Leadbeater. *The Christian Creed*, pp. 56-57.

of the Spirit instead of with the eyes of the flesh, we should not weep over a form, which is a corpse giving back the materials out of which it was builded, but we should joy over the life passing onwards into nobler form, to expand under the unchanging process the powers still latent within.

Through that perpetual sacrifice of the Logos all lives exist; it is the life by which the universe is ever becoming. This life is One, but it embodies itself in myriad forms, ever drawing them together and gently overcoming their resistance. Thus it is an At-one-ment, a unifying force, by which the separated lives are gradually made conscious of their unity, labouring to develop in each a self-consciousness, which shall at last know itself to be one with all others, and its root One and divine.

This is the primary and ever-continued sacrifice, and it will be seen that it is an outpouring of Life directed by Love, a voluntary and glad pouring forth of Self for the making of other Selves. This is " the joy of thy Lord " [1] into which the faithful servant enters, significantly followed by the statement that He was hungry, thirsty, naked, sick, a stranger and in prison, in the helped or neglected children of men. To the free Spirit to give itself is joy, and it feels its life the more keenly the more it pours itself forth. And the more it gives the more it grows, for the law of the growth of life is that it increases by pouring itself forth and not by drawing from without—by giving, not by taking. Sacrifice, then, in its primary meaning, is a thing of joy; the Logos

[1] St. Matt., xxv, 21, 23, 31-45.

pours Himself out to make a world, and, seeing the travail of His soul, is satisfied.[1]

But the word has come to be associated with suffering, and in all religious rites of sacrifice some suffering, if only that of a trivial loss to the sacrificer, is present. It is well to understand how this change has come about, so that when the word " sacrifice " is used the instinctive connotation is one of pain.

The explanation is seen when we turn from the manifesting Life to the forms in which it is embodied, and look at the question of sacrifice from the side of the forms. While the life of Life is in giving, the life, or persistence, of form is in taking, for the form is wasted as it is exercised, it is diminished as it is exerted. If the form is to continue, it must draw fresh material from outside itself in order to repair its losses, else will it waste and vanish away. The form must grasp, keep, build into itself what it has grasped, else it can not persist; and the law of growth of the form is to take and assimilate that which the wider universe supplies. As the consciousness identifies itself with the form, regarding the form as itself, sacrifice takes on a painful aspect; to give, to surrender, to lose what has been acquired, is felt to undermine the persistence of the form, and thus the Law of Sacrifice becomes a law of pain instead of a law of joy.

Man had to learn by the constant breaking up of forms, and the pain involved in the breaking, that he must not identify himself with the wasting and changing

[1] Isa., liii, 11.

forms, but with the growing persistent life, and he was taught his lesson not only by external nature, but by the deliberate lessons of the Teachers who gave him religions.

We can trace in the religions of the world four great stages of instruction in the Law of Sacrifice. First, man was taught to sacrifice part of his material possession in order to gain increased material prosperity, and sacrifices were made in charity to men and in offerings to Deities, as we may read in the scriptures of the Hindus, the Zoroastrians, the Hebrews, indeed all the world over. The man gave up something he valued to insure future prosperity to himself, his family, his community, his nation. He sacrificed in the present to gain in the future. Secondly, came a lesson a little harder to learn; instead of physical prosperity and worldly good, the fruit to be gained by sacrifice was celestial bliss. Heaven was to be won, happiness was to be enjoyed on the other side of death—such was the reward for sacrifices made during the life led on earth.

A considerable step forward was made when a man learned to give up the things for which his body craved for the sake of a distant good which he could not see nor demonstrate. He learned to surrender the visible for the invisible, and in so doing rose in the scale of being; for so great is the fascination of the visible and the tangible, that if a man be able to surrender them for the sake of an unseen world in which he believes, he has acquired much strength and has made a long step towards the realization of that unseen world. Over and over again martyrdom has been endured, obloquy has been faced, man has learned to stand alone, bearing all that his race could pour upon him of pain, misery, and shame, looking to that which is beyond the grave. True, there still remains in this a longing for celestial glory, but it is no small thing to be able to stand alone on earth and rest on spiritual companionship, to cling firmly to the inner life when the outer is all torture.

The third lesson came when a man, seeing himself as part of a greater life, was willing to sacrifice himself for the good of the whole, and so became strong enough to recognize that sacrifice was right, that a part, a fragment, a unit in the sum total of life, should subordinate the part to the whole, the fragment to the totality. Then he learned to do right, without being affected by the outcome to his own person, to do duty, without wishing for result to himself, to endure because endurance was right, not because it would be crowned, to give because gifts were due to humanity, not because they would be repaid by the Lord. The hero-soul thus trained was ready for the fourth lesson; that sacrifice of all the separated fragment possesses is to be offered because the Spirit is not really separate but is part of the divine Life, and knowing no difference, feeling no separation, the man pours himself forth as part of the Life Universal, and in the expression of that Life he shares the joy of his Lord.

It is in the three earlier stages that the pain-aspect of sacrifice is seen. The first meets but small sufferings; in the second the physical life and all that earth has to give may be sacrificed; the third is the great time of testing, of trying, of the growth and evolution of the human soul. For in that stage duty may demand all in which life seems to consist, and the man, still identified in *feeling* with the form, though *knowing* himself theoretically to transcend it, finds that all he feels as life is demanded of him, and questions: " If I let this go, what then will remain? " It seems as though consciousness itself would cease with this surrender, for it must lose its hold on all it realizes, and it sees nothing to grasp on the other side. An over-mastering conviction, an imperious voice, call on him to surrender his very life. If he shrinks back, he must go on in the life of sensation, the life of the intellect, the life of the world, and as he has the joys he dared not resign, he finds a constant dissatisfaction, a constant craving, a constant regret and lack of pleasure in the world, and he realizes the truth of the saying of the Christ, that " he that will save his life shall lose it," [1] and that the life that was loved and clung to is only lost at last. Whereas if he risks all in obedience to the voice that summons, if he throws away his life, then in losing it, he finds it unto life eternal,[2] and he discovers that the life he surrendered was only death in life, that all he gave up was illusion, and that he found reality. In that choice the metal of the soul is proved, and only the pure gold comes forth from the fiery furnace, where life seemed to be surrendered but where life was won. And then follows the joyous discovery that the life thus won is won for all,.

[1] St. Matt., xvi, 25.   [2] St. John, xii, 25.

not for the separated self, that the abandoning of the separated self has meant the realizing of the Self in man, and that the resignation of the limit which alone seemed to make life possible has meant the pouring out into myriad forms, an undreamed vividness and fulness, " the powers of an endless life." [1]

Such is an outline of the Law of Sacrifice, based on the primary Sacrifice of the Logos, that Sacrifice of which all other sacrifices are reflections.

We have seen how the man Jesus, the Hebrew disciple, laid down His body in glad surrender that a higher Life might descend and become embodied in the form. He thus willingly sacrificed, and how by that act He became a Christ of full stature, to be the Guardian of Christianity, and to pour out His life into the great religion founded by the Mighty One with whom the sacrifice had identified Him. We have seen the Christ-Soul passing through the great Initiations—born as a little child, stepping down into the river of the world's sorrows, with the waters of which he must be baptized into his active ministry, transfigured on the Mount, led to the scene of his last combat, and triumphing over death. We have now to see in what sense he is an atonement, how in the Christ-life the Law of Sacrifice finds perfect expression.

The beginning of what may be called the ministry of the Christ come to manhood is in that intense and permanent sympathy with the world's sorrows which is typified by the stepping down into the river. From

[1] Heb., vii, 16.

that time forward the life must be summed up in the phrase, " He went about doing good "; for those who sacrifice the separated life to be a channel of the divine Life, can have no interest in this world save the helping of others. He learns to identify himself with the consciousness of those around him, to feel as they feel, think as they think, enjoy as they enjoy, suffer as they suffer, and thus he brings into his daily waking life that sense of unity with others which he experiences in the higher realms of being. He must develop a sympathy which vibrates in perfect harmony with the many-toned chord of human life, so that he may link in himself the human and the divine lives, and become a mediator between heaven and earth.

Power is now manifested in him, for the Spirit is resting on him, and he begins to stand out in the eyes of men as one of those who are able to help their younger brethren to tread the path of life. As they gather round him, they feel the power that comes out from him, the divine Life in the accredited Son of the Highest. The souls that are hungry come to him and he feeds them with the bread of life; the diseased with sin approach him, and he heals them with the living word which cures the sickness and makes whole the soul; the blind with ignorance draw nigh him, and he opens their eyes by the light of his wisdom. It is the chief mark in his ministry that the lowest and the poorest, the most desperate and the most degraded, feel in approaching him no wall of separation, feel as they throng around him welcome and not repulsion; for there radiates from him a love that understands and that can therefore never wish to repel. However low the soul may be, he never feels the Christ-Soul as standing above him but rather as standing beside him, treading with human feet the ground he also treads; yet as filled with some strange uplifting power that raises him upwards and fills him also with new impulse and fresh inspiration.

Thus he lives and labours, a true Saviour of men, until the time comes when he must learn another lesson, losing for a while his consciousness of that divine Life of which his own has been becoming ever more and more the expression. And this lesson is that the true centre of divine Life lies within and not without. The Self has its centre within each human soul—truly is " the centre everywhere," for Christ is *in* all, and God in Christ—and no embodied life, nothing " out of the Eternal " [1] can help him in his direct need. He has to learn that the true unity of Father and Son is to be found within and not without, and this lesson can only come in uttermost isolation, when he feels forsaken by the God outside himself. As this trial approaches, he cries out to those who are nearest to him to watch with him through his hour of darkness; and then, by the breaking of every human sympathy, the failing of every human love, he finds himself thrown back on the life of the divine Spirit, and cries out to his Father, feeling himself in conscious union with Him, that the cup may pass away. Having stood alone, save for that divine

[1] *Light on the Path*, § 8.

Helper, he is worthy to face the last ordeal, where the God without him vanishes, and only the God within is left. " My God, my God, why hast Thou forsaken me? " rings out the bitter cry of startled love and fear. The last loneliness descends on him, and he feels himself forsaken and alone. Yet never is the Father nearer to the Son than at the moment when the Christ-Soul feels himself forsaken, for as he thus touches the lowest depth of sorrow, the hour of his triumph begins to dawn. For now he learns that he must himself become the God to whom he cries, and by feeling the last pang of separation he finds the eternal unity, he feels the fount of life is within, and knows himself eternal.

None can become fully a Saviour of men nor sympathize perfectly with all human suffering, unless he has faced and conquered pain and fear and death unaided, save by the aid he draws from the God within him. It is easy to suffer when there is unbroken consciousness between the higher and the lower; nay, suffering is not, while that consciousness remains unbroken, for the light of the higher makes darkness in the lower impossible, and pain is not pain when borne in the smile of God. There is a suffering that men have to face, that every Saviour of man must face, where darkness is on the human consciousness, and never a glimmer of light comes through; he must know the pang of the despair felt by the human soul when there is darkness on every side, and the groping consciousness cannot find a hand to clasp. Into that darkness every Son of Man goes down, ere he rises triumphant; that bitterest experience

11

is tasted by every Christ, ere he is " able to save them to the uttermost " [1] who seek the Divine through him.

Such a one has become truly divine, a Saviour of men, and he takes up the world-work for which all this has been the preparation. Into him must pour all the forces that make against man, in order that in him they may be changed into forces that help. Thus he becomes one of the Peace-centres of the world, which transmute the forces of combat that would otherwise crush man. For the Christs of the world are these Peace-centres into which pour all warring forces, to be changed within them and then poured out as forces that work for harmony.

Part of the sufferings of the Christ not yet perfect lies in this harmonizing of the discord-making forces in the world. Although a Son, he yet learns by suffering and is thus " made perfect." [2] Humanity would be far more full of combat and rent with strife were it not for the Christ-disciples living in its midst, and harmonizing many of the warring forces into peace.

When it is said that the Christ suffers " for men ", that His strength replaces their weakness, His purity their sin, His wisdom their ignorance, a truth is spoken; for the Christ so becomes one with men that they share with Him and He with them. There is no substitution of Him for them, but the taking of their lives into His, and the pouring of His life into theirs. For, having risen to the plane of unity, He is able to share all He has gained, to give all He has won. Standing above

[1] Heb., vii. 25.   [2] *Ibid.*, v, 8, 9.

the plane of separateness and looking down at the souls immersed in separateness, He can reach each while they cannot reach each other. Water can flow from above into many pipes, open to the reservoir though closed as regards each other, and so He can send His life into each soul. Only one condition is needed in order that a Christ may share His strength with a younger brother: that in the separated life the human consciousness will open itself to the divine, will show itself receptive of the offered life, and take the freely outpoured gift. For so reverent is God to that Spirit which is Himself in man, that He will not even pour into the human soul a flood of strength and life unless that soul is willing to receive it. There must be an opening from below as well as an outpouring from above, the receptiveness of the lower nature as well as the willingness of the higher to give. That is the link between the Christ and the man; that is what the churches have called the outpouring of " divine grace "; that is what is meant by the " faith " necessary to make the grace effective. As Giordano Bruno once put it—the human soul has windows, and can shut those windows close. The sun outside is shining, the light is unchanging; let the windows be opened and the sunlight must stream in. The light of God is beating against the windows of every human soul, and when the windows are thrown open, the soul becomes illuminated. There is no change in God, but there is a change in man; and man's will may not be forced, else were the divine Life in him blocked in its due evolution.

Thus in every Christ that rises, all humanity is lifted a step higher and by His wisdom the ignorance of the whole world is lessened. Each man is less weak because of His strength, which pours out over all humanity and enters the separated soul. Out of that doctrine, seen narrowly, and therefore mis-seen, grew the idea of the vicarious Atonement as a legal transaction between God and man, in which Jesus took the place of the sinner. It was not understood that One who had touched that height was verily one with all His brethren; identity of nature was mistaken for a personal substitution, and thus the spiritual truth was lost in the harshness of a judicial exchange.

Then he comes to a knowledge of his place in the world, of his function in nature—to be Saviour and to make atonement for the sins of the people. He stands in the inner Heart of the world, the Holy of Holies, as a High Priest of Humanity. He is one with all his brethren, not by a vicarious substitution, but by the unity of a common life. Is any sinful? He is sinful in them, that his purity may purge them. Is any sorrowful? In them he is the man of sorrows; every broken heart breaks his, in every pierced heart his heart is pierced. Is any glad? In them he is joyous, and pours out his bliss. Is any craving? In them he is feeling want that he may fill them with his utter satisfaction. He has everything, and because it is his it is theirs. He is perfect; then they are perfect with him. He is strong; who then can be weak, since he is in them? He climbed to his high place that he might pour out to all below him, and he lives in order that all may share his life. He lifts the whole world with him as he rises, the path is easier for all men, because he has trodden it. " Every son of man may become such a manifested Son of God, such a Saviour of the world. In each such Son is ' God manifest in the flesh ', [1] the atonement that aids all mankind, the living power that makes all things new. Only one thing is needed to bring that power into manifested activity in any individual soul; the soul must open the door and let Him in. Even He, all-permeating, cannot force His way against His brother's will; the human will can hold its own alike against God and man, and by the law of evolution it must voluntarily associate itself with divine action, and not be broken into sullen submission. Let the will throw open the door, and the life will flood the soul. While the door is closed it will only gently breathe through it its unutterable fragrance, that the sweetness of that fragrance may win, where the barrier may not be forced by strength.

" This it is, in part, to be a Christ; but how can mortal pen mirror the immortal, or mortal words tell of that which is beyond the power of speech? Tongue may not utter, the unillumined mind may not grasp, that mystery of the Son who has become one with the Father, carrying in His bosom the sons of men." [2]

Those who would prepare to rise to such a life in the future must begin even now to tread in the lower life the path of the Shadow of the Cross. Nor should they

---

[1] I. Tim., iii, 16.

[2] A. Besant. *Theosophical Review*, Dec., 1988, pp. 344, 345.

doubt their power to rise, for to do so is to doubt the God within them. " Have faith in yourself," is one of the lessons that comes from the higher view of man, for that faith is really in the God within. There is a way by which the shadow of the Christ-life may fall on the common life of man, and that is by doing every act as a sacrifice, not for what it will bring to the doer but for what it will bring to others, and, in the daily common life of small duties, petty actions, narrow interests, by changing the motive and thus changing all. Not one thing in the outer life need necessarily be varied; in any life sacrifice may be offered, amid any surroundings God may be served. Evolving spirituality is marked not by what a man does, but by how he does it; not in the circumstances, but in the attitude of a man towards them, lies the opportunity of growth. " And indeed this symbol of the cross may be to us as a touchstone to distinguish good from the evil in many of the difficulties of life. ' Only those actions through which shines the light of the cross are worthy of the life of the disciple,' says one of the verses in a book of occult maxims; and it is interpreted to mean that all that the aspirant does should be prompted by the fervour of self-sacrificing love. The same thought appears in a later verse: ' When one enters the path, he lays his heart upon the cross; when the cross and the heart have become one, then hath he reached the goal.' So, perchance, we may measure our progress by watching whether selfishness or self-sacrifice is dominant in our lives."[1]

[1] C. W. Leadbeater. *The Christian Creed*, pp. 61, 62.

Every life which begins thus to shape itself is preparing the cave in which the Child-Christ shall be born, and the life shall become a constant at-one-ment, bringing the divine more and more into the human. Every such life shall grow into the life of a " beloved Son ", and shall have in it the glory of the Christ. Every man may work in that direction by making every act and power a sacrifice, until the gold is purged from the dross, and only the pure ore remains.

CHAPTER VIII

RESURRECTION AND ASCENSION

THE doctrines of the Resurrection and Ascension of Christ also form part of the Lesser Mysteries, being integral portions of " The Solar Myth ", and of the life-story of the Christ in man.

As regards Christ Himself they have their historical basis in the facts of His continuing to teach His apostles after His physical death, and of His appearance in the Greater Mysteries as Hierophant after His direct instructions had ceased, until Jesus took His place. In the mythic tales the resurrection of the hero and his glorification invariably formed the conclusion of his death-story; and in the Mysteries, the body of the candidate was always thrown into a death-like trance, during which he, as a liberated soul, travelled through the invisible world, returning and reviving the body after three days. And in the life-story of the individual, who is becoming a Christ, we shall find, as we study it, that the dramas of the Resurrection and Ascension are repeated.

But before we can intelligently follow that story, we must master the outlines of the human constitution, and understand the natural and spiritual bodies of man.

" There is a natural body, and there is a spiritual body." [1]

There are still some uninstructed people who regard man as a mere duality, made up of " soul " and " body ". Such people use the words " soul " and " spirit " as synonyms, and speak indifferently of " soul and body ", or " spirit and body ", meaning that man is composed of two constituents, one of which perishes at death, while the other survives. For the very simple and ignorant this rough division is sufficient, but it will not enable us to understand the mysteries of the Resurrection and Ascension.

Every Christian who has made even a superficial study of the human constitution recognizes in it three distinct constituents—Spirit, Soul, and Body. This division is sound, though needing further subdivision for more profound study, and it has been used by St. Paul in his prayer that " your whole spirit and soul and body be preserved blameless." [2] That threefold division is accepted in Christian Theology.

The Spirit itself is really a Trinity, the reflection and image of the Supreme Trinity, and this we shall study in the following chapter.[3] The true man, the immortal, who is the Spirit, is the Trinity in man. This is life, consciousness, and to this the spiritual body belongs, each aspect of the Trinity having its own Body. The Soul is dual, and comprises the mind and the emotional nature, with its appropriate garments. And the

[1] I. Cor., xv, 44.   [2] I. Thess., v, 23.
[3] See Chapter IX, " The Trinity."

Body is the material instrument of Spirit and Soul. In one Christian view of man he is a twelve-fold being, six modifications forming the spiritual man, and six the natural man; according to another, he is divisible into fourteen, seven modification of consciousness and seven corresponding types of form. This latter view is practically identical with that studied by Mystics and it is usually spoken of as seven-fold, because there are really seven divisions, each being two-fold, having a life-side and a form-side.

The word body means a vehicle of consciousness, or an instrument of consciousness; that in which consciousness is carried about, as in a vehicle, or which consciousness uses to contact the external world, as a mechanic uses an instrument. Or, we may liken it to a vessel, in which consciousness is held, as a jar holds liquid. It is a form used by a life, and we know nothing of consciousness save as connected with such forms. The form may be of rarest, subtlest, materials, may be so diaphanous that we are only conscious of the indwelling life; still it is there, and it is composed of Matter. It may be so dense that it hides the indwelling life, and we are conscious only of the form; still the life is there, and it is composed of the opposite of Matter—Spirit. The student must study and re-study this fundamental fact—the duality of all manifested existence, the inseparable co-existence of Spirit and Matter in a grain of dust, in the Logos, the God manifested. The idea must become part of him; else must he give up the study of the Lesser Mysteries. The Christ, as God and Man, only shows out on the kosmic scale the same fact of duality that is repeated everywhere in nature. On that original duality everything in the universe is formed.

Man has a " natural body," and this is made up of four different and separable portions, and is subject to death. Two of these are composed of physical matter, and are never completely separated from each other until death, though a partial separation may be caused by anæsthetics, or by disease. These two may be classed together as the Physical Body. In this the man carries on the conscious activities while he is awake; speaking technically, it is his vehicle of consciousness in the physical world.

The third portion is the Desire Body, so called because man's feeling and passional nature finds in this its special vehicle. In sleep, the man leaves the physical body, and carries on his conscious activities in this, which functions in the invisible world closest to our visible earth. It is therefore his vehicle of consciousness in the lowest of the superphysical worlds, which is also the first world into which men pass at death.

The fourth portion is the Mental Body, so called because man's intellectual nature, so far as it deals with the concrete, functions in this. It is his vehicle of consciousness in the second of the superphysical worlds, which is also the second, or lower heavenly world, into which men pass after death, when freed from the world alluded to in the preceding paragraph.

These four portions of his encircling form, made up of the dual physical body, the desire body, and the mental body, form the natural body of which St. Paul speaks.

This scientific analysis has fallen out of the ordinary Christian teaching, which is vague and confused on this matter. It is not that the churches have never possessed it; on the contrary, this knowledge of the constitution of man formed part of the teachings in the Lesser Mysteries; the simple division into Spirit, Soul, and Body was exoteric, the first rough and ready division given as a foundation. The sub-division as regards the " Body " was made in the course of later instruction, as a preliminary to the training by which the instructor enabled his pupil to separate one vehicle from another, and to use each as a vehicle of consciousness in its appropriate region.

This conception should be readily enough grasped. If a man wants to travel on the solid earth, he uses as his vehicle an automobile or a train. If he wants to travel on the liquid seas, he changes his vehicle, and takes a ship. If he wants to travel in the air, he changes his vehicle again and uses an airplane. He is the same man throughout, but he is using three different vehicles, according to the kind of matter he wants to travel in. The analogy is rough and inadequate, but it is not misleading. When a man is busy in the physical world, his vehicle is the physical body, and his consciousness works in and through that body. When he passes into the world beyond the physical, in sleep and at death, his vehicle is the desire body, and he may learn to use this consciously, as he uses the physical consciously. He already uses it unconsciously every day of his life when he is feeling and desiring, as well as every night of his life. When he goes on into the heavenly world after death, his vehicle is the mental body, and this also he is daily using, when he is thinking, and there would be no thought in the brain were there none in the mental body.

Man has further " a spiritual body ". This is made up of three separable portions, each portion belonging to one of, and separating off, the three Persons in the Trinity of the human Spirit. St. Paul speaks of being " caught up to the third heaven ", and of there hearing " unspeakable words which it is not lawful for a man to utter." [1] These different regions of the invisible supernal worlds are known to Initiates, and they are well aware that those who pass beyond the first heaven need that truly spiritual body as their vehicle, and that according to the development of its three divisions is the heaven into which they can penetrate.

The lowest of these three divisions is usually called the Causal Body, for a reason that will be only fully assimilable by those who have studied the teaching of Reincarnation—taught in the Early Church—and who understand that human evolution needs very many successive lives on earth, ere the germinal soul of the undeveloped man can become the perfected soul of the Christ, and then, becoming perfect as the Father in Heaven,[2] can realize the union of the Son with the Father.[3]

---

[1] II. Cor., xii, 2, 4. 　　　　　[2] St. Matt., v, 48.
[3] St. John, xvii, 22, 23.

It is a body that lasts from life to life, and in it all memory of the past is stored. From it come forth the causes that build up the lower bodies. It is the receptacle of human experience, the treasure-house in which all we gather in our lives is stored up, the seat of Conscience, the wielder of the Will.

The second of the three divisions of the spiritual body is spoken of by St. Paul in the significant words: " We have a building of God, an house not made with hands, eternal in the heavens." [1] That is the Bliss Body, the glorified body of the Christ, " the Resurrection body ". It is not a body which is " made with hands ", by the working of consciousness in the lower vehicles; it is not formed by experience, not builded out of the materials gathered by man in his long pilgrimage. It is a body which belongs to the Christ-life, the life of Initiation; to the divine unfoldment in man; it is builded of God, by the activity of the Spirit, and grows during the whole life or lives of the Initiate, only reaching its perfection at " the Resurrection ".

The third division of the spiritual body is the fine film of subtle matter that separates off the individual Spirit as a Being, and yet permits the interpenetration of all by all, and is thus the expression of the fundamental unity. In the day when the Son Himself shall " be subject unto him that put all things under him, that God may be all in all," [2] this film will be transcended, but for us it remains the highest division of the

[1] II. Cor., v, 1.
[2] I. Cor., xv, 28.

spiritual body, in which we ascend to the Father, and are united with Him.

Christianity has always recognized the existence of three worlds, or regions, through which a man passes; first, the physical world; secondly, an intermediate state into which he passes at death; thirdly, the heavenly world. These three worlds are universally believed in by educated Christians; only the uninstructed imagine that a man passes from his death-bed into the final state of beatitude. But there is some difference of opinion as to the nature of the intermediate world. The Roman Catholic names it Purgatory, and believes that every soul passes into it, save that of the Saint, the man who has reached perfection, or that of a man who has died in "mortal sin". The great mass of humanity pass into a purifying region, wherein a man remains for a period varying in length according to the sins he has committed, only passing out of it into the heavenly world when he has become pure. The various communities that are called Protestant vary in their teachings as to details, and mostly repudiate the idea of *post mortem* purification; but they agree broadly that there is an intermediate state, sometimes spoken of as "Paradise", or as a "waiting period". The heavenly world is almost universally, in modern Christendom, regarded as a final state, with no very definite or general idea as to its nature, or as to the progress or stationary condition of those attaining to it. In early Christianity this heaven was considered to be, as it really is, a stage in the progress of the soul, reincarnation in one form or another, the pre-existence of the soul, being then very generally taught. The result was, of course, that the heavenly state was a temporary condition, though often a very prolonged one, lasting for " an age "—as stated in the Greek of the New Testament, the age being ended by the return of the man for the next stage of his continuing life and progress—and not "everlasting", as in the mistranslation of the English authorized version.[1]

In order to complete the outline necessary for the understanding of the Resurrection and Ascension, we must see how these various bodies are developed in the higher evolution.

The physical body is in a constant state of flux, its minute particles being continually renewed, so that it is ever building; and as it is composed of the food we eat, the liquids we drink, the air we breathe, and particles drawn from our physical surroundings, both people and things, we can steadily purify it, by choosing its materials well, and thus make it an ever purer vehicle through which to act, receptive of subtler vibrations, responsive to purer desires, to nobler and more elevated thoughts. For this reason all who aspired to attain to the Mysteries were subjected to rules of diet, ablution, etc., and were desired to be very careful as to the people with whom they associated, and the places to which they went.

[1] This mistranslation was a very natural one, as the translation was made in the seventeenth century, and all idea of the pre-existence of the soul and of its evolution had long faded out of Christendom, save in the teachings of a few sects regarded as heretical and persecuted by the Roman Catholic Church.

The desire body also changes, in similar fashion, but the materials for it are expelled and drawn in by the play of the desires, arising from the feelings, passions, and emotions. If these are coarse, the materials built into the desire body are also coarse, while as these are purified, the desire body grows subtle and becomes very sensitive to the higher influences. In proportion as a man dominates his lower nature, and becomes unselfish in his wishes, feelings, and emotions, as he makes his love for those around him less selfish and grasping, he is purifying this higher vehicle of consciousness; the result is that when out of the body in sleep he has higher, purer and more instructive experiences, and when he leaves the physical body at death, he passes swiftly through the intermediate state, the desire body disintegrating with great rapidity, and not delaying him on his onward journey.

The mental body is similarly being built now, in this case by thoughts. It will be the vehicle of consciousness in the heavenly world, but is being built now by aspirations, by imagination, reason, judgment, artistic faculties, by the use of all the mental powers. Such as the man makes it, so must he wear it, and the length and richness of his heavenly state depend on the kind of mental body he has built during his life on earth.

As a man enters the higher evolution, this body comes into independent activity on this side of death, and he gradually becomes conscious of his heavenly life, even amid the whirl of mundane existence. Then he becomes

12

" the Son of man which is in heaven ",[1] who can speak with the authority of knowledge on heavenly things. When the man begins to live the life of the Son, having passed on to the Path of Holiness, he lives in heaven while remaining on earth, coming into conscious possession and use of this heavenly body. And inasmuch as heaven is not far away from us, but surrounds us on every side, and we are only shut out from it by our incapacity to feel its vibrations, not by their absence; inasmuch as those vibrations are playing upon us at every moment of our lives; all that is needed to be in Heaven is to become conscious of those vibrations. We become conscious of them with the vitalizing, the organizing, the evolution of this heavenly body, which, being built out of the heavenly materials, answers to the vibrations of the matter of the heavenly world. Hence the " Son of man " is ever in heaven. But we know that the " Son of man " is a term applied to the Initiate, not to the Christ risen and glorified but to the Son while he is yet " being made perfect ".[2]

During the stages of evolution that lead up to and include the Probationary Path, the first division of the spiritual body—the Causal Body—develops rapidly, and enables the man, after death, to rise into the second heaven. After the Second Birth, the birth of the Christ in man, begins the building of the Bliss Body " in the heavens ". This is the body of the Christ, developing during the day of His service on earth, and, as it develops, the consciousness of the " Son of God "

[1] St. John, iii, 13.   [2] Heb., v, 9.

becomes more and more marked, and the coming union with the Father illuminates the unfolding Spirit.

In the Christian Mysteries—as in the ancient Egyptian, Chaldæan, and others—there was an outer symbolism which expressed the stages through which the man was passing. He was brought into the chamber of Initiation, and was stretched on the ground with his arms extended, sometimes on a cross of wood, sometimes merely on the stone floor, in the posture of a crucified man. He was then touched with the thyrsus on the heart—the " spear " of the crucifixion—and, leaving the body, he passed into the worlds beyond, the body falling into a deep trance, the death of the crucified. The body was placed in a sarcophagus of stone, and there left, carefully guarded. Meanwhile the man himself was treading first the strange obscure regions called "the heart of the earth", and thereafter the heavenly mount, where he put on the perfected bliss body, now fully organized as a vehicle of consciousness. In that he returned to the body of flesh, to reanimate it. The cross bearing that body, or the entranced and rigid body, if no cross had been used, was lifted out of the sarcophagus and placed on a sloping surface, facing the east, ready for the rising of the sun on the third day. At the moment that the rays of the sun touched the face, the Christ, the perfected Initiate or Master, re-entered the body, glorifying it by the bliss body He was wearing, changing the body of flesh by contact with the body of bliss, giving it new properties, new powers, new capacities, transmuting it into His own likeness. That was the Resurrection of the Christ, and thereafter the body of flesh itself was changed, and took on a new nature.

This is why the sun has ever been taken as the symbol of the rising Christ, and why, in Easter hymns, there is constant reference to the rising of the Sun of Righteousness. So also is it written of the triumphant Christ: " I am He that liveth and was dead; and behold, I am alive for evermore, Amen; and have the keys of hell and of death." [1] All the powers of the lower worlds have been taken under the dominion of the Son, who has triumphed gloriously: over Him death no more has power, " He holdeth life and death in His strong hand." [2] He is the risen Christ, the Christ triumphant.

The Ascension of the Christ was the Mystery of the third part of the spiritual body, the putting on of the Vesture of Glory, preparatory to the union of the Son with the Father, of man with God, when the Spirit re-entered the glory it had " before the world was ".[3] Then the triple Spirit becomes one, knows itself eternal, and the Hidden God is found. That is imaged in the doctrine of the Ascension, so far as the individual is concerned.

The Ascension for humanity is when the whole race has attained the Christ condition, the state of the Son, and that Son becomes one with the Father, and God is

[1] Rev., i, 18.
[2] H. P. Blavatsky, *The Voice of the Silence*, p. 90, 5th ed.
[3] St. John, xvii, 5.

all in all. That is the goal, prefigured in the triumph of the Initiate, but reached only when the human race is perfected, and when " the great orphan Humanity " is no longer an orphan, but consciously recognizes itself as the Son of God.

Thus studying the doctrines of the Atonement, the Resurrection, and the Ascension, we reach the truth unfolded concerning them in the Lesser Mysteries, and we begin to understand the full truth of the apostolic teaching that Christ was not a unique personality, but " the first fruits of them that slept,"[1] and that every man was to become a Christ. Not then was the Christ regarded as an external Saviour, by whose imputed righteousness men were to be saved from divine wrath. There was current in the Church the glorious and inspiring teaching that He was but the first fruits of humanity, the model that every man should reproduce in himself, the life that all should share. The Initiates have ever been regarded as these first fruits, the promise of a race made perfect. To the early Christian, Christ was the living symbol of his own divinity, the glorious fruit of the seed he bore in his own heart. Not to be saved by an external Christ, but to be glorified into an inner Christ, was the teaching of esoteric Christianity, of the Lesser Mysteries. The stage of discipleship was to pass into that of Sonship. The life of the Son was to be lived among men till it was closed by the Resurrection, and the glorified Christ became one of the perfected Saviours of the world.

[1] I. Cor., xv, 20.

How far greater a Gospel than the one of modern days! Placed beside that grandiose ideal of esoteric Christianity, the exoteric teaching of the churches seems narrow and poor indeed.

CHAPTER IX

THE TRINITY

ALL fruitful study of the Divine Existence must start from the affirmation that it is One. All the Sages have thus proclaimed It; every religion has thus affirmed It; every philosophy thus posits It—" One only without a second." [1] "Hear, O Israel!" cried Moses, "The Lord our God is one Lord." [2] "To us there is but one God," [3] declares St. Paul. "There is no God but God," affirms the founder of Islam, and makes the phrase the symbol of his faith. One Existence unbounded, known in Its fulness only to Itself—the word It seems more reverent and inclusive than He, and is therefore used. That is the Eternal Darkness, out of which is born the Light.

But as the Manifested God, the One appears as Three. A Trinity of Divine Beings, One as God, Three as manifested Powers. This also has ever been declared, and the truth is so vital in its relation to man and his evolution that it is one which ever forms an essential part of the Lesser Mysteries.

Among the Hebrews, in consequence of their anthropomorphizing tendencies, the doctrine was kept secret,

[1] *Chandogyopanishat*, VI, ii, 1.

[2] Deut., vi, 4.   [3] I. Cor., viii, 6.

but the Rabbis studied and worshipped the Ancient of Days, from whom came forth the Wisdom, from whom the Understanding—Kether, Chochmah, Binah, these formed the Supreme Trinity, the shining forth in time of the One beyond time. The book of the Wisdom of Solomon refers to this teaching, making Wisdom a Being. " According to Maurice, ' The first Sephira, who is denominated Kether the Crown, Kadmon the pure Light, and En Soph the Infinite,[1] is the omnipotent Father of the universe. . . . The second is the Chochmah, whom we have sufficiently proved, both from sacred and Rabbinical writings, to be the creative Wisdom. The third is the Binah, or heavenly Intelligence, whence the Egyptians had their Cneph, and Plato his *Nous Demiurgos*. He is the Holy Spirit who . . . pervades, animates and governs this boundless universe.' " [2]

The bearing of this doctrine on Christian teaching is indicated by Dean Milman in his *History of Christianity*. He says: " This Being (the Word or the Wisdom) was more or less distinctly impersonated, according to the more popular or more philosophic, the more material or the more abstract, notions of the age or people. This was the doctrine from the Ganges, or even the shores of the Yellow Sea, to the Ilissus; it was the fundamental principle of the Indian religion and the Indian philosophy; it was the basis of Zoroastrianism; it was pure

[1] An error: En Soph or Ain Soph is not one of the Trinity, but the One Existence, manifested in the Three; nor is Kadmon, or Adam Kadmon, one Sephira, but their totality.

[2] Quoted in Williamson's *The Great Law*, pp. 201, 202.

Platonism; it was the Platonic Judaism of the Alexandrian school. Many fine passages might be quoted from Philo on the impossibility that the first self-existing Being should become cognizable to the sense of man; and even in Palestine, no doubt, John the Baptist, and our Lord Himself spoke no new doctrine, but rather the common sentiment of the more enlightened, when they declared ' that no man had seen God at any time.' In conformity with this principle the Jews, in the interpretation of the older Scriptures, instead of direct and sensible communication from the one great Deity, had interposed either one or more intermediate beings as the channels of communication. According to one accredited tradition alluded to by St. Stephen, the law was delivered ' by the disposition of angels '; according to another this office was delegated to a single angel, sometimes called the Angel of the Law (see Gal., iii, 19); at others the Metatron. But the more ordinary representative, as it were, of God, to the sense and mind of man, was the Memra, or the Divine Word; and it is remarkable that the same appellation is found in the Indian, the Persian, the Platonic, and the Alexandrian systems. By the Targumists, the earliest Jewish commentators on the Scriptures, this term had been already applied to the Messiah; nor is it necessary to observe the manner in which it has been sanctified by its introduction into the Christian scheme." [1]

As above said by the learned Dean, the idea of the Word, the Logos, was universal, and it formed part of

[1] H. H. Milman, *The History of Christianity*, 1867, pp. 70-72.

the idea of a Trinity.   Among the Hindus, the philosophers speak of the manifested Brahman as Sat-Chit-Ananda—Existence, Intelligence, and Bliss.   Popularly, the Manifested God is a Trinity; Shiva, the Beginning and the End; Vishnu, the Preserver; Brahmâ, the Creator of the Universe.   The Zoroastrian faith presents a similar Trinity: Ahuramazadao, the Great One, the First; then " the twins ", the dual Second Person—for the Second Person in a Trinity is ever dual, deteriorated in modern days into an opposing God and Devil—and the Universal Wisdom, Armaiti.   In Northern Buddhism we find Amitabha, the boundless Light; Avalokiteshvara the source of incarnations, and the Universal Mind, Mandjusri.   In Southern Buddhism the idea of God has faded away, but with significant tenacity the triplicity reappears as that in which the Southern Buddhist takes his refuge—the Buddha, the Dharma (the Doctrine), the Sangha (the Order).   But the Buddha Himself is sometimes worshipped as a Trinity; on a stone in Buddha Gaya is inscribed a salutation to Him as an incarnation of the Eternal One, and it is said: " Om! Thou art Brahma, Vishnu, and Mahesha (Shiva) . . . I adore Thee, who art celebrated by a thousand names and under various forms, in the shape of Buddha, the God of Mercy." [1]

In extinct religions the same idea of a Trinity is found. In Egypt it dominated all religious worship.   " We have a hieroglyphical inscription in the British Museum as early as the reign of Senechus of the eighth century

[1] *Asiatic Researches*, i, 285.

before the Christian era, showing that the doctrine of Trinity in Unity already formed part of their religion." [1] This is true of a far earlier date. Ra, Osiris, and Horus formed one widely worshipped Trinity; Osiris, Isis, and Horus were worshipped at Abydos; other names are given in different cities, and the triangle is the frequently used symbol of the Triune God. The idea which underlay these Trinities, however named, is shown in a passage quoted from Marutho, in which an oracle, rebuking the pride of Alexander the Great, speaks of: " First God, then the Word, and with Them the Spirit." [2]

In Chaldæa, Anu, Ea, and Bel were the Supreme Trinity, Anu being the Origin of all, Ea the Wisdom, and Bel the creative Spirit. Of China, Williamson remarks: " In ancient China the emperors used to sacrifice every third year to ' Him who is one and three.' There was a Chinese saying, ' Fo is one person but has three forms.' . . . In the lofty philosophical system known in China as Taoism, a trinity also figures: ' Eternal Reason produced One, One produced Two, Two produced Three, and Three produced all things,' which, as Le Compte goes on to say, ' seems to show as if they had some knowledge of the Trinity '." [3]

In the Christian doctrine of the Trinity we find a complete agreement with other faiths as to the functions of the three Divine Persons, the word Person coming

---

[1] S. Shapre. *Egyptian Mythology and Egyptian Christology*, p. 14.

[2] See Williamson's *The Great Law*, p. 196.

[3] *Loc. cit.*, pp. 208, 209.

from *persona*, a mask, that which covers something, the mask of the One Existence, Its Self-revelation under a form. The Father is the Origin and End of all; the Son is dual in His nature, and is the Word, or the Wisdom; the Holy Spirit is the Creative Intelligence, that brooding over the chaos of primeval matter organizes it into the materials out of which forms can be constructed.

It is this identity of functions under so many varying names which shows that we have here not a mere outer likeness, but an expression of an inner truth. There is something of which this triplicity is a manifestation, something that can be traced in nature and in evolution, and which, being recognized, will render intelligible the growth of man, the stages of his evolving life. Further, we find that in the universal language of symbolism the Persons are distinguished by certain emblems, and may be recognized by these under diversity of forms and names.

But there is one other point that must be remembered ere we leave the exoteric statement of the Trinity—that in connection with all these Trinities there is a fourth fundamental manifestation, the Power of the God, and this has always a feminine form. In Hinduism each person in the Trinity has His manifested Power, the One and these six aspects making up the sacred Seven. With many of the Trinities one feminine form appears, then ever specially connected with the Second Person, and then there is the sacred Quaternary.

Let us now see the inner truth.

The One becomes manifest as the First Being, the Self-Existent Lord, the Root of all, the Supreme Father; the word Will, or Power, seems best to express this primary Self-revealing, since until there is Will to manifest there can be no manifestation, and until there is Will manifested, impulse is lacking for further unfoldment. The universe may be said to be rooted in the divine Will. Then follows the second aspect of the One—Wisdom; Power is guided by Wisdom, and therefore it is written that "without him was not any thing made that was made "[1]; Wisdom is dual in its nature, as will presently be seen. When the aspects of Will and Wisdom are revealed, a third aspect must follow to make them effective—Creative Intelligence, the divine mind in Action. A Jewish prophet writes: "He hath made the earth by his Power, he hath established the world by his Wisdom; and hath stretched out the heaven by his Understanding,"[2] the reference to the three functions being very clear.[3] These Three are inseparable, indivisible, three aspects of One. Their functions may be thought of separately, for the sake of clearness, but cannot be disjoined. Each is necessary to each, and each is present in each. In the First Being, Will, Power, is seen as predominant, as characteristic, but Wisdom and Creative Action are also present; in the Second Being, Wisdom is seen as predominant, but Power and Creative Action are none the less inherent in Him; in the Third

[1] St. John, i, 3.
[2] Jer., li, 15.
[3] See *Ante*, pp. 124, 125.

Being, Creative Action is seen as predominant, but Power and Wisdom are ever also to be seen. And though the words First, Second, Third are used, because the Beings are thus manifested in Time, in the order of Self-unfolding, yet in Eternity they are known as interdependent and co-equal, " None is greater or less than Another."[1]

This Trinity is the divine Self, the divine Spirit, the Manifested God, He that " was and is and is to come," [2] and He is the root of the fundamental triplicity in life, in consciousness.

But we saw that there was a Fourth Person, or in some religions a second Trinity, feminine, the Mother. This is That which makes manifestation possible, That which eternally in the One is the root of limitation and division, and which, when manifested, is called Matter. This is the divine Not-Self, the divine Matter, the manifested Nature. Regarded as One, She is the Fourth, making possible the activity of the Three, the Field of Their operations by virtue of Her infinite divisibility, at once the " Handmaid of the Lord," [3] and also His Mother, yielding of Her substance to form His Body, the universe, when overshadowed by His power.[4] Regarded carefully She is seen to be triple also, existing in three inseparable aspects, without which She could not be. These are Stability—Inertia or Resistance—Motion, and Rhythm; the fundamental or essential

---

[1] Athanasian Creed.
[2] Rev., iv, 8.   [3] St. Luke, 38.
[4] Ibid., 35.

qualities of Matter, these are called. They alone render Spirit effective, and have therefore been regarded as the manifested Powers of the Trinity. Stability or Inertia affords a basis, the fulcrum for the lever; Motion is then rendered manifest, but could make only chaos; then Rhythm is imposed, and there is Matter in vibration, capable of being shaped and moulded. When the three qualities are in equilibrium, there is the One, the Virgin Matter, unproductive. When the power of the Highest overshadows Her, and the breath of the Spirit comes upon Her, the qualities are thrown out of equilibrium, and She becomes the divine Mother of the worlds.

The first interaction is between Her and the Third Person of the Trinity; by His action She becomes capable of giving birth to form. Then is revealed the Second Person; who clothes Himself in the material thus provided, and becomes the Mediator, linking in His own Person, Spirit and Matter, the Archetype of all forms. Only through Him does the First Person become revealed as the Father of all Spirits.

It is now possible to see why the Second Person of the Trinity of Spirit is ever dual; He is the One who clothes Himself in Matter, in whom the twin-halves of Deity appear in union, not as one. Hence also is He Wisdom; for Wisdom on the side of Spirit is the Pure Reason that knows itself as the One Self and knows all things in that Self, and on the side of Matter it is Love, drawing the infinite diversity of forms together, and making each form a unit, not a mere heap of particles

—the principle of attraction which holds the worlds and all in them in a perfect order and balance. This is the Wisdom which is spoken of as " mightily and sweetly ordering all things," [1] which sustains and preserves the universe.

In the world-symbols, found in every religion, the Point—that which has position only—has been taken as a symbol of the First Person in the Trinity. On this symbol St. Clement of Alexandria remarks that we abstract from a body its properties, then depth, then breadth, then length; " the point which remains is a unit, so to speak, having position: from which if we abstract position, there is the conception of unity."[2] He shines out, as it were, from the infinite Darkness, a Point of Light, the centre of a future universe, a Unit, in whom all exists inseparate; the matter which is to form the universe, the field of His work, is marked out by the backward and forward vibration of the Point in every direction, a vast sphere, limited by His Will, His Power. This is the making of " the earth by His Power ", spoken of by Jeremiah.[3] Thus the full symbol is a Point within a sphere, represented usually as a Point within a circle. The Second Person is represented by a Line, a diameter of this circle, a single complete vibration of the Point, and this Line is equally in every direction within the sphere; this Line dividing the circle in

[1] Book of Wisdom, viii, 1.

[2] Vol. IV.   Ante-Nicene Library.   St. Clement of Alexandria, *Stromata*, bk. V, ch. ii.

[3] See *Ante*, 181.

twain signifies also His duality, that in Him Matter and Spirit—a unity in the First Person—are visibly two, though in union. The Third Person is represented by a Cross formed by two diameters at right angles to each other within the circle, the second line of the Cross separating the upper part of the circle from the lower. This is the Greek Cross.[1]

When the Trinity is represented as a Unity, the Triangle is used, either inscribed within a circle, or free. The universe is symbolized by two triangles interlaced, the Trinity of Spirit with the apex of the triangle upward, the Trinity of Matter with the apex of the triangle downward, and if colours are used, the first is white, yellow, golden or flame-coloured, and the second black, or some dark shade.

The kosmic process can now be readily followed. The One has become Two, and the Two Three, and the Trinity is revealed. The Matter of the universe is marked out and awaits the action of Spirit. This is the " in the beginning " of Genesis, when " God created the heaven and the earth," [2] a statement further elucidated by the repeated phrases that He " laid the foundations of the earth " [3]; we have here the marking out of the material, but a mere chaos, " without form and void." [4]

On this begins the action of the Creative Intelligence, the Holy Spirit, who " moved upon the face of the

---

[1] See *Ante*, p. 143. [2] Gen., i, 1.

[3] Job, xxxviii, 4; Zech., xii, 1; etc.

[4] Gen., i, 2.

13

waters," [1] the vast ocean of matter. Thus His was the first activity, though He was the Third Person—a point of great importance.

In the Mysteries this work was shown in its detail as the preparation of the matter of the universe, the formation of atoms, the drawing of these together into aggregates, and the grouping of these together into elements, and of these again into gaseous, liquid, and solid compounds. This work includes not only the kind of matter called physical, but also all the subtle states of matter in the invisible worlds. He further as the " Spirit of Understanding " conceived the forms into which the prepared matter should be shaped, not building the forms, but by the action of the Creative Intelligence producing the ideas of them, the heavenly prototypes, as they are often called. This is the work referred to when it is written, He " stretched out the heaven by His Understanding." [2]

The work of the Second Person follows that of the Third. He by virtue of His Wisdom " established the world," [3] building all globes and all things upon them, " all things were made by him." [4] He is the organizing Life of the worlds, and all beings are rooted in Him.[5] The life of the Son thus manifested in the matter prepared by the Holy Spirit—again the great " Myth " of the Incarnation—is the life that builds up, preserves, and maintains all forms, for He is the Love, the attracting

[1] Gen.
[2] See *Ante*, p. 181.   [3] See *Ante*, p. 181.
[4] St. John, i, 3.   [5] *Bhagavad Gita*, ix, 4.

power, that gives cohesion to forms, enabling them to grow without falling apart, the Preserver, the Supporter, the Saviour. That is why all must be subject to the Son,[1] all must be gathered up in Him, and why " no man cometh unto the Father but by " Him.[2]

For, the work of the First Person follows that of the Second; as that of the Second follows that of the Third. He is spoken of as " the Father of Spirits," [3] the " God of the Spirits of all flesh," [4] and His is the gift of the divine Spirit, the true Self in man. The human Spirit is the outpoured divine Life of the Father, poured into the vessel prepared by the Son, out of the materials vivified by the Spirit. And this Spirit in man, being from the Father—from whom came forth the Son and the Holy Spirit—is a Unity like Himself, with the three aspects in One, and man is thus truly made " in our image, after our likeness," [5] and is able to become " perfect, even as your Father which is in heaven is perfect." [6]

Such is the kosmic process, and in human evolution it is repeated: " as above, so below."

The Trinity of the Spirit in man, being in the divine likeness, must show out the divine characteristics, and thus we find in him Power, which, whether in its higher form of Will or its lower form of Desire, gives the impulse to his evolution. We find also in him Wisdom,

---

[1] I Cor., xv, 27, 28.

[2] St. John, xiv, 6. See also the further meaning of this text on p. 186.

[3] Heb., xii, 9.   [4] Num., xvi, 22.

[5] Gen., i, 26.   [6] St. Matt., v, 48,

the Pure Reason which has Love as its expression in the world of forms, and lastly Intelligence, or Mind, the active shaping energy. And in man also we find that the manifestation of these in his evolution is from the third to the second, and from the second to the first. The mass of humanity is unfolding the mind, evolving the intelligence, and we can see its separative action everywhere, isolating, as it were, the human atoms and developing each severally, so that they may be fit materials for building up a divine Humanity. To this point only has the race arrived, and here it is still working.

As we study a small minority of our race we see that the second aspect of the divine Spirit in man is appearing, and we speak of it in Christendom as the Christ in man. Its evolution lies, as we have seen, beyond the first of the Great Initiations, and Wisdom and Love are the marks of the Initiate, shining out more and more as he develops this aspect of the Spirit. Here again is it true that " no man cometh to the Father but by me ", for only when the life of the Son is touching on completion can He pray: " Now, O Father, glorify Thou me with thine own self, with the glory which I had with thee before the world was." [1] Then the Son ascends to the Father and becomes one with Him in the divine glory; He manifests self-existence, the existence inherent in his divine nature, unfolded from seed to flower, for " as the Father hath life in himself, so hath he given to the Son to have life in himself." [2] He

[1] St. John, xvii, 5.
[2] St. John, v, 26.

becomes a living self-conscious Centre in the Life of
God, a Centre able to exist as such, no longer bound
by the limitations of his earlier life, expanding to divine
consciousness, while keeping the identity of his life un-
shaken, a living, fiery Centre in the divine Flame.

In this evolution now lies the possibility of divine Incarnation in the future, as this evolution in the past has
rendered possible divine Incarnations in our own world.
These living Centres do not lose Their identity, nor the
memory of Their past, of aught that They have experienced in the long climb upwards; and such a Self-conscious Being can come forth from the Bosom of the
Father, and reveal Himself for the helping of the world.
He has maintained the union in Himself of Spirit and
Matter, the duality of the Second Person—all divine
Incarnations in all religions are therefore connected with
the Second Person in the Trinity—and hence can readily
reclothe Himself for the physical manifestation, and
again become Man. This nature of the Mediator He
has retained, and is thus a link between the celestial and
terrestrial Trinities, " God with us " [1] He has ever been
called.

Such a Being, the glorious fruit of a past universe,
can come into the present world with all the perfection
of His divine Wisdom and Love, with all the memory of
His past, able by virtue of that memory to be the perfect
Helper of every living Being, knowing every stage because He has lived it, able to help at every point because
He has experienced all. " In that He Himself hath

[1] St. Matt., i, 22.

suffered being tempted, He is able to succour them that are tempted." [1]

It is in the humanity behind Him that lies this possibility of divine Incarnation; He comes down, having climbed up, in order to help others to climb the ladder. And as we understand these truths, and something of the meaning of the Trinity, above and below, what was once a mere hard unintelligible dogma becomes a living and vivifying truth. Only by the existence of the Trinity in man is human evolution intelligible, and we see how man evolves the life of the intellect and then the life of the Christ. On that fact mysticism is based, and our sure hope that we shall know God. Thus have the Sages taught, and as we tread the Path they show, we find that their testimony is true.

[1] Heb., ii, 18.

CHAPTER X

PRAYER[1]

SOME people are antagonistic to prayer, failing to see any causal nexus between the uttering of a petition and the happening of an event, whereas the religious spirit is as strongly attached to it, and finds its very life in prayer. Yet even the religious man sometimes feels uneasy as to the rationale of prayer; is he teaching the All-wise, is he urging beneficence on the All-Good, is he altering the will of Him in " whom is no variableness, neither shadow of turning "?[2] Yet he finds in his own experience and in that of others " answers to prayer," a definite sequence of a request and a fulfilment.

Many of these do not refer to subjective experiences, but to hard facts of the so-called objective world. A man has prayed for money, and the post has brought him the required amount; a woman has prayed for food, and food has been brought to her door. In connection with charitable undertakings, especially, there is plenty of evidence of help prayed for in urgent need, and of

[1] Much of this chapter has already appeared in an earlier work by the author, entitled, *Some Problems of Life*.

[2] St. James, i, 17.

speedy and liberal response. On the other hand, there is also plenty of evidence of prayers left unanswered; of the hungry starving to death, of the child snatched from its mother's arms by disease, despite the most passionate appeals to God. Any true view of prayer must take into account all these facts.

Nor is this all. There are many facts in this experience which are strange and puzzling. A prayer that perhaps is trivial meets with an answer, while another on an important matter fails; a passing trouble is relieved, while a prayer poured out to save a passionately beloved life finds no response. It seems almost impossible for the ordinary student to discover the law according to which a prayer is or is not productive.

The first thing necessary in seeking to understand this law is to analyse prayer itself, for the word is used to cover various activities of the consciousness, and prayers cannot be dealt with as though they formed a simple whole. There are prayers which are petitions for definite worldly advantages, for the supply of physical necessities—prayers for food, clothing, money, employment, success in business, recovery from illness, etc. These may be grouped together as Class A. Then we have prayers for help in moral and intellectual difficulties and for spiritual growth—for the overcoming of temptations, for strength, for insight, for enlightenment. These may be grouped as Class B. Lastly, there are the prayers that ask for nothing, that consist in meditation on and adoration of the divine Perfection, in intense aspiration for union with God—the ecstasy of the mystic, the meditation of the sage, the soaring rapture of the saint. This is the true " communion between the Divine and the human", when the man pours himself out in love and veneration for THAT which is inherently attractive that compels the love of the heart. These we will call Class C.

In the invisible worlds there exist many kinds of Intelligences, which come into relationship with man, a veritable Jacob's ladder, on which the Angels of God ascend and descend, and above which stands the Lord Himself.[1] Some of these Intelligences are mighty spiritual Powers, others are exceedingly limited beings, inferior in consciousness to man. This occult side of Nature—of which more will presently be said [2]—is a fact, recognized by all religions. All the world is filled with living things, invisible to fleshly eyes. The invisible worlds interpenetrate the visible, and crowds of intelligent beings throng round us on every side. Some of these are accessible to human requests, and others are amenable to the human will. Christianity recognizes the existence of the higher classes of Intelligences under the general name of Angels, and teaches that they are " ministering spirits, sent forth to minister " [3]; but what is their ministry, what the nature of their work, what their relationship to human beings, all that was part of the instruction given in the Lesser Mysteries, as the actual communication with them was enjoyed in the Greater; but in

[1] Gen., xxviii, 12, 13.
[2] See Chapter xii.
[3] Heb., i, 14.

modern days these truths have sunk into the background, except the little that is taught in the Greek and Roman communions. For the Protestant, " the ministry of angels " is little more than a phrase.

In addition to all these, man is himself a constant creator of invisible beings. Vibrations of his thoughts and desires create forms of subtle matter the only life of which is the thought or the desire which ensouls them; he thus creates an army of invisible servants, who range through the invisible worlds seeking to do his will. Yet, again, there are in these worlds human helpers, who work there in their subtle bodies while their physical bodies are sleeping, whose attentive ear may catch a cry for help. And to crown all, there is the ever-present, ever-conscious Life of God Himself, potent and responsive at every point of His realm, of Him without whose knowledge not a sparrow falleth to the ground,[1] not a dumb creature thrills in joy or pain, not a child laughs or sobs —that all-pervading, all-embracing, all-sustaining Life and Love, in which we live and move.[2]

As nought that can give pleasure or pain can touch the human body without the sensory nerves carrying the message of its impact to the brain-centres, and as there thrills down from those centres through the motor nerves the answer that welcomes or repels, so does every vibration in the universe, which is His body, touch the consciousness of God, and draw thence responsive action. Nerve-cells, nerve-threads, and muscular fibres may be

[1] St. Matt., x, 29.
[2] Acts., xvii, 28.

the agents of feeling and moving, but it is the *man* that feels and acts; so may myriads of Intelligences be the agents, but it is God who knows and answers. Nothing can be so small as not to affect that delicate omnipresent consciousness, nothing so vast as to transcend it.

We are so limited that the very idea of such an all-embracing consciousness staggers and confounds us; yet perhaps a gnat might be as confounded if he tried to measure the consciousness of Pythagoras. Professor Huxley, in a remarkable passage, has imagined the possibility of the existence of beings rising higher and higher in intelligence, the consciousness ever expanding, and the reaching of a stage as much above the human as the human is above that of the black-beetle.[1] That is not a flight of the scientific imagination, but a description of a fact. There is a Being whose consciousness is present at every point of His universe, and therefore can be affected from any point. That consciousness is not only vast in its field, but inconceivably acute, not diminished in delicate capacity to respond because it stretches its vast area in every direction, but it is more responsive than a more limited consciousness, more perfect in understanding than the more restricted. So far from it being the case that the more exalted the Being the more difficult would it be to reach His consciousness, the very reverse is true. The more exalted the Being, the more easily is His consciousness affected.

[1] T. H. Huxley. *Essays on Some Controverted Questions*, p. 36.

Now this all-pervading Life is everywhere utilizing as channels all the embodied lives to which He has given birth, and any one of them may be used as an agent of that all-conscious Will. In order that that Will may express itself in the outer world, a means of expression must be found, and these beings, in proportion to their receptivity, offer the necessary channels, and become the intermediary workers between one point of the kosmos and another. They act as the motor nerves of His body, and bring about the required action.

Let us now take the classes into which we have divided prayers, and see the methods by which they will be answered.

When a man utters a prayer of Class A there are several means by which his prayer may be answered. Such a man is simple in his nature, with a conception of God natural, inevitable, at the stage of evolution in which he is; he regards Him as the supplier of his own needs, in close and immediate touch with his daily necessities, and he turns to Him for his daily bread as naturally as a child turns to his father or mother. A typical instance of this is the case of George Müller, of Bristol, before he was known to the world as a philanthropist, when he was beginning his charitable work, and was without friends or money. He prayed for food for the children who had no resource save his bounty, and money always came sufficient for the immediate needs. What had happened? His prayer was a strong energetic desire, and that desire creates a form, of which it is the life and directing energy. That vibrating, living creature has but one idea, the idea that ensouls it—help is wanted, food is wanted; and it ranges the subtle world, seeking. A charitable man desires to give help to the needy, is seeking opportunity to give. As the magnet to soft iron, so is such a person to the desire-form, and it is attracted to him. It rouses in his brain vibrations identical with its own—George Müller, his orphanage, its needs—and he sees the outlet for his charitable impulse, draws a cheque, and sends it. Quite naturally Müller would say that God put it into the heart of such a one to give the needed help. In the deepest sense of the words that is true, since there is no life, no energy, in His universe that does not come from God; but the intermediate agency, according to the divine laws, is the desire-form created by the prayer.

The result could be obtained equally well by a deliberate exercise of the will, without any prayer by a person who understood the mechanism concerned, and the way to put it in motion. Such a man would think clearly of what he needed, would draw to him the kind of subtle matter best suited to his purpose to clothe the thought and by a deliberate exercise of his will would either send it to a definite person to represent his need, or to range his neighbourhood and be attracted by a charitably disposed person. There is here no prayer, but a conscious exercise of will and knowledge.

In the case of most people, however, ignorant of the forces of the invisible worlds and unaccustomed to exercise their wills, the concentration of mind and the earnest desire which are necessary for successful action are far more easily reached by prayer than by a deliberate mental effort to put forth their own strength. They would doubt their own power, even if they understood the theory, and doubt is fatal to the exercise of the will. That the person who prays does not understand the machinery he sets going in no wise affects the result. A child who stretches out his hand and grasps an object need not understand anything of the working of the muscles, nor of the electrical and chemical changes set up by the movement in muscles and nerves, nor need he elaborately calculate the distance of the object by measuring the angle made by the optic axes; he wills to take hold of the thing he wants and the apparatus of his body obeys his will though he does not even know of its existence. So is it with the man who prays, unknowing of the creative force of his thought, of the living creature he has sent out to do his bidding. He acts as unconsciously as the child, and like the child grasps what he wants. In both cases God is equally the primal Agent, all power being from Him; in both cases the actual work is done by the apparatus provided by His laws.

But this is not the only way in which prayers of this class are answered. Some one temporarily out of the physical body and at work in the invisible worlds, or a passing Angel, may hear the cry for help, and may then put the thought of sending the required aid into the brain of some charitable person. " The thought of So-and-so came into my head this morning", such a person will say. " I dare say a cheque would be useful to him."

Very many prayers are answered in this way, the link between the need and the supply being some invisible Intelligence. Herein is part of the ministry of the lower angels, and they will thus supply personal necessities, as well as bring aid to charitable undertakings.

The failure of prayers of this class is due to another hidden cause. Every man has contracted debts which have to be paid; his wrong thoughts, wrong desires and wrong actions have built up obstacles in his way, and sometimes even hem him in as the walls of a prison-house. A debt of wrong is discharged by a payment of suffering; a man must bear the consequences of the wrongs he has wrought. We are living in a realm of law, and forces may be modified or entirely frustrated by the play of other forces with which they come into contact. Two exactly similar forces might be applied to two exactly similar balls; in one case, one other force might be applied to the ball, and it might strike the mark aimed at; in the other, a second force might strike the ball and send it entirely out of its course. And so with two similar prayers: one may go on its way, unopposed and effect its object; the other may be flung aside by the far stronger force of a past wrong. One prayer is answered, the other unanswered; but in both cases the result is by law.

Let us consider Class B. Prayers for help in moral and intellectual difficulties have a double result: they act directly to attract help, and they react on the person who prays. They draw the attention of the Angels, of the disciples working outside the body, who are ever seeking to help the bewildered mind, and counsel, encouragement, illumination, are thrown into the brain-consciousness, thus giving the answer to prayer in the most direct way. " And he kneeled down and prayed . . . and there appeared an angel unto him from heaven, strengthening him." [1] Ideas are suggested which clear away an intellectual difficulty, or throw light on an obscure moral problem, or the sweetest comfort is poured into the distressed heart, soothing its perturbations and calming its anxieties.

There is also what is sometimes called a subjective answer to such prayers, the reaction of the prayer on the utterer. His prayer places his heart and mind in the receptive attitude, and this stills the lower nature, and thus allows the strength and illuminative power of the higher to stream into it unchecked. The currents of energy which normally flow downwards, or outwards, from the Inner Man, are, as a rule, directed to the external world, and are utilized in the ordinary affairs of life by the brain-consciousness, for the carrying on of its daily activities. But when this brain-consciousness turns away from the outer world, and shutting its outward-going doors, directs its gaze inwards; when it deliberately closes itself to the outer and opens itself to the inner; then it becomes a vessel able to receive and to hold, instead of a mere conduit-pipe between the interior and exterior worlds. In the silence obtained by the cessation of the noises of external activities, the " still small voice " of the Spirit can make itself heard, and the

[1] St. Luke, xxii, 41, 43.

concentrated attention of the expectant mind enables
it to catch the soft whisper of the Inner Self.

Even more markedly does help come from without
and from within, when the prayer is for spiritual enlightenment, for spiritual growth. Not only do all helpers,
angelic and human, most eagerly seek to forward spiritual progress, seizing on every opportunity offered by
the upward-aspiring soul; but the longing for such
growth liberates energy of a high kind, the spiritual
longing calling forth an answer from the spiritual realm.
Once more the law of sympathetic vibrations asserts
itself, and the note of lofty aspiration is answered by a
note of its own order, by a liberation of energy of its
own kind, by a vibration synchronous with itself. The
divine Life is ever pressing from above against the limits
that bind it, and when the upward-rising force strikes
against those limits from below, the separating wall is
broken through, and the divine Life floods the Soul.
When a man feels that inflow of spiritual life, he cries:
" My prayer has been answered, and God has sent down
His Spirit into my heart." Truly so; yet he rarely
understands that that Spirit is ever seeking entrance,
but that coming to His own, His own receive Him not.[1]
" Behold, I stand at the door, and knock: if any man
hear my voice, and open the door, I will come in to
him."[2]

The general principle with regard to all prayers of
this class is that just in proportion to the submergence

[1] St. John, i, 11.
[2] Rev., iii, 20.

14

of the personality and the intensity of the upward aspiration will be the answer from the wider life within and without us. We separate ourselves. If we cease the separation and make ourselves one with the greater, we find that light and life and strength flow into us. When the separate will is turned away from its own objects and set to serve the divine purpose, then the strength of the Divine pours into it. As a man swims against the stream, he makes slow progress; but with it, he is carried on by all the force of the current. In every department of Nature the divine energies are working, and everything that a man does he does by means of the energies that are working in the line along which he desires to do; his greatest achievements are wrought, not by his own energies, but by the skill with which he selects and combines the forces that aid him, and neutralizes those that oppose him by those that are favourable. Forces that would whirl us away as straws in the wind become our most effective servants when we work with them. Is it then any wonder that in prayer, as in everything else, the divine energies become associated with the man who, by his prayer, seeks to work as part of the Divine?

The highest form of prayer in Class B merges almost imperceptibly into Class C, where prayer loses its petitionary character, and becomes either a meditation on, or a worship of, God. Meditation is the steady quiet fixing of the mind on God, whereby the lower mind is stilled and presently left vacant, so that the Spirit, escaping from it, rises into contemplation of the divine

Perfection, and reflects within himself the divine Image.
" Meditation is silent or *unuttered* prayer, or as Plato
expressed it: ' the ardent turning of the Soul towards
the Divine; not to ask any particular good (as in the
common meaning of prayer), but for good itself, for the
Universal Supreme Good '." [1]

This is the prayer that, by thus liberating the Spirit,
is the means of union between man and God. By the
working of the laws of thought a man becomes that
which he thinks, and when he meditates on the divine
perfections he gradually reproduces in himself that on
which his mind is fixed. Such a mind, shaped to the
higher and not the lower, cannot bind the Spirit, and
the freed Spirit leaping upward to his source, prayer is
lost in union and separateness is left behind.

Worship also, the rapt adoration from which all petition is absent, and which seeks to pour itself forth in
sheer love of the Perfect, dimly sensed, is a means—the
easiest means—of union with God. In this the consciousness, limited by the brain, contemplates in mute
ecstasy the Image it creates of Him whom it knows to
be beyond imagining, and oft, rapt by the intensity of
his love beyond the limits of the intellect, the man as a
free Spirit soars upwards into realms where these limits
are transcended, and feels and knows far more than on
his return he can tell in words or clothe in form.

Thus the mystic gazes on the Beatific Vision; thus
the sage rests in the calm of the Wisdom that is beyond
knowledge; thus the saint reaches the purity wherein

[1] H. P. Blavatsky. *Key to Theosophy*, p. 10.

God is seen. Such prayer irradiates the worshipper, and from the mount of such high communion descending to the plains of earth, the very face of flesh shines with supernal glory, translucent to the flame that burns within. Happy they who know the reality which no words may convey to those who know it not. Those whose eyes have seen " the King in His beauty " [1] will remember, and they will understand.

When prayer is thus understood, its perennial necessity for all who believe in religion will be patent, and we see why its practice has been so much advocated by all who study the higher life. For the student of the Lesser Mysteries prayer should be of the kinds grouped under Class B, and he should endeavour to rise to the pure meditation and worship of the last class, eschewing altogether the lower kinds. For him the teaching of Iamblichus on this subject is useful. Iamblichus says that prayers " produce an indissoluble and sacred communion with the Gods," and then proceeds to give some interesting details on prayer, as considered by the practical Occultist. " For this is of itself a thing worthy to be known, and renders more perfect the science concerning the Gods. I say, therefore, that the first species of prayers is Collective; and that it is also the leader of contact with, and a knowledge of, divinity. The second species is the bond of concordant Communion, calling forth, prior to the energy of speech, the gifts imparted by the Gods, and perfecting the whole of our operations prior to our intellectual conceptions. And the third

[1] Isa., xxxiii, 17.

and most perfect species of prayer is the seal of ineffable Union with the divinities, in whom it establishes all the power and authority of prayer; and thus causes the soul to repose in the Gods, as in a never-failing port. But from these three terms, in which all the divine measures are contained, suppliant adoration not only conciliates to us the friendship of the Gods, but supernally extends to us three fruits, being as it were three Hesperian apples of gold. The first of these pertains to illumination; the second to a communion of operation; but through the energy of the third we receive a perfect plenitude of divine fire. . . . No operation, however, in sacred concerns, can succeed without the intervention of prayer. Lastly, the continual exercise of prayer nourishes the vigour of our intellect, and renders the receptacle of the soul far more capacious for the communications of the Gods. It likewise is the divine key, which opens to men the penetralia of the Gods; accustoms us to the splendid rivers of supernal light; in a short time perfects our inmost recesses, and disposes them for the ineffable embrace and contact of the Gods; and does not desist till it raises us to the summit of all. It also gradually and silently draws upward the manners of our soul, by divesting them of everything foreign to a divine nature, and clothes us with the perfections of the Gods. Besides this, it produces an indissoluble communion and friendship with divinity, nourishes a divine love, and inflames the divine part of the soul. Whatever is of an opposing and contrary nature in the soul, it expiates and purifies; expels whatever is prone to generation and retains anything of the dregs of mortality in its ethereal and splendid spirit; perfects a good hope and faith concerning the reception of divine light; and in one word, renders those by whom it is employed the familiars and domestics of the Gods." [1]

Out of such study and practice one inevitable result arises, as a man begins to understand, and as the wider range of human life unfolds before him. He sees that by knowledge his strength is much increased, that there are forces around him that he can understand and control, and that in proportion to his knowledge is his power. Then he learns that Divinity lies hidden within himself, and that nothing that is fleeting can satisfy that God within; that only union with the One, the Perfect, can still his cravings. Then there gradually arises within him the will to set himself at one with the Divine; he ceases to seek vehemently to change circumstances, and to throw fresh causes into the stream of effects. He recognizes himself as an agent rather than an actor, a channel rather than a source, a servant rather than a master, and seeks to discover the divine purposes and to work in harmony therewith.

When a man has reached that point, he has risen above all prayer, save that which is meditation and worship; he has nothing to ask for, in this world or in any other; he remains in a steadfast serenity, seeking but to serve God. That is the state of Sonship, where the will of the Son is one with the will of the Father, where the one calm surrender is made, " Lo, I come to

[1] *On the Mysteries*, sec. v, ch. 26.

do Thy will, O God.   I am content to do it; yea, Thy
law is within my heart." [1]   Then all prayer is seen to
be unnecessary; all asking is felt as an impertinence;
nothing can be longed for that is not already in the
purposes of that Will, and all will be brought into active
manifestations as the agents of that Will perfect themselves in the work.

[1] Ps., xl, 7, 8, Prayer Book version.

CHAPTER XI

THE FORGIVENESS OF SINS

" I BELIEVE in . . . the forgiveness of sins." " I acknowledge one baptism for the remission of sins." The words fall facilely from the lips of worshippers in Christian churches throughout the world, as they repeat the familiar creeds called those of the Apostles and the Nicene. Among the sayings of Jesus the words frequently recur: " Thy sins are forgiven thee ", and it is noteworthy that this phrase constantly accompanies the exercise of His healing powers, the release from physical and moral disease being thus marked as simultaneous. In fact, on one occasion He pointed to the healing of a palsy-stricken man as a sign that he had a right to declare to a man that his sins were forgiven.[1] So also of one woman it was said: " Her sins, which are many, are forgiven, for she loved much." [2] In the famous Gnostic treatise, the *Pistis Sophia*, the very purpose of the Mysteries is said to be the remission of sins. " Should they have been sinners, should they have been in all the sins and all the iniquities of the world, of which I have spoken unto you, nevertheless if they turn themselves

[1] St. Luke, v, 18-26.
[2] St. Luke, vii, 47.

and repent, and have made the renunciation which I have just described unto you, give ye unto them the mysteries of the kingdom of light; hide them not from them at all. It is because of sin that I have brought these mysteries into the world, for the remission of all the sins which they have committed from the beginning. Wherefore have I said unto you aforetime, ' I came not to call the righteous.' Now, therefore, I have brought the mysteries, that the sins of all men may be remitted, and they be brought into the kingdom of light. For these mysteries are the boon of the first mystery of the destruction of the sins and iniquities of all sinners." [1]

In these Mysteries, the remission of sin is by baptism, as in the acknowledgement in the Nicene Creed. Jesus says: " Hearken, again, that I may tell you the word in truth, of what type is the mystery of baptism which remitteth sins. . . . When a man receiveth the mysteries of the baptisms, those mysteries become a mighty fire, exceedingly fierce, wise, which burneth up all sins; they enter into the soul occultly, and devour all the sins which the spiritual counterfeit hath implanted in it." And after describing further the process of purification, Jesus adds: " This is the way in which the mysteries of the baptisms remit sins and every iniquity." [2]

In one form or another the " forgiveness of sins " appears in most, if not in all, religions; and wherever this consensus of opinion is found, we may safely conclude, according to the principle already laid down, that

[1] G. R. S. Mead, translated. *Loc. cit.*, bk. ii, §§ 260, 261.
[2] *Ibid.*, §§ 299, 300.

some fact in nature underlies it. Moreover, there is a response in human nature to this idea that sins are forgiven; we notice that people suffer under a consciousness of wrong-doing, and that when they shake themselves clear of their past, and free themselves from the shackling fetters of remorse, they go forward with glad heart and sunlit eyes, though erstwhile enclouded by darkness. They feel as though a burden were lifted off them, a clog removed. The " sense of sin " has disappeared, and with it the gnawing pain. They know the springtime of the soul, the word of power which makes all things new. A song of gratitude wells up as the natural outburst of the heart, the time for the singing of birds is come, there is " joy among the Angels." This not uncommon experience is one that becomes puzzling, when the person experiencing it, or seeing it in another, begins to ask himself what has really taken place, what has brought about the change in consciousness, the effects of which are so manifest.

Modern thinkers, who have thoroughly assimilated the idea of changeless laws underlying all phenomena, and who have studied the workings of these laws, are at first apt to reject any and every theory of the forgiveness of sins as being inconsistent with that fundamental truth, just as the scientist, penetrated with the idea of the inviolability of law, repels all thought which is inconsistent with it. And both are right in founding themselves on the unfaltering working of law, for law is but the expression of the divine Nature, in which there is no variableness, neither shadow of turning. Any view of the forgiveness of sins that we may adopt must not clash with this fundamental idea, as necessary to ethical as to physical science. " The bottom would fall out of everything " if we could not rest securely in the everlasting arms of the Good Law.

But in pursuing our investigations, we are struck with the fact that the very Teachers who are most insistent on the changeless working of law are also those who emphatically proclaim the forgiveness of sins. At one time Jesus is saying: " That every idle word that men shall speak, they shall give account thereof in the day of judgment," [1] and at another: " Son, be of good cheer, thy sins be forgiven." [2] So in the *Bhagavad Gita* we read constantly of the bonds of action, that " the world is bound by action," [3] and that a man " recovereth the characteristics of his former body " [4]; and yet it is said that " even if the most sinful worship me, with undivided heart, he, too, must be accounted righteous." [5] It would seem, then, that whatever may have been intended in the world's Scriptures by the phrase, " the forgiveness of sins ", it was not thought, by Those who best know the law, to clash with the inviolable sequence of cause and effect.

If we examine even the crudest idea of the forgiveness of sins prevalent in our own day, we find that the believer in it does not mean that the forgiven sinner is to escape the consequences of his sin in this world; the

[1] St. Matt., xii, 36.   [2] *Ibid.*, ix, 2.
[3] *Loc. cit.*, iii, 9.   [4] *Ibid.*, vi, 43.
[5] *Ibid.*, ix, 30.

drunkard, whose sins are forgiven on his repentance, is still seen to suffer from shaken nerves, impaired digestion, and the lack of confidence shown towards him by his fellow-men. The statements made as to forgiveness, when they are examined, are ultimately found to refer to the relations between the repentant sinner and God, and to the *post-mortem* penalties attached to unforgiven sin in the creed of the speaker, and not to any escape from the mundane consequences of sin. The loss of belief in reincarnation, and of a sane view as to the continuity of life, whether it were spent in this or in the next two worlds [1] brought with it various incongruities and indefensible assertions, among them the blasphemous and terrible idea of the eternal torture of the human soul for sins committed during the brief span of one life spent on earth. In order to escape from this nightmare, theologians posited a forgiveness which should release the sinner from this dread imprisonment in an eternal hell. It did not, and was never supposed to, set him free in this world from the natural consequences of his ill-doings, nor—except in modern Protestant communities—was it held to deliver him from prolonged purgatorial sufferings, the direct results of sin, after the death of the physical body. The law had its course, both in this world and in purgatory, and in each world sorrow followed on the heels of sin, even as the wheels follow the ox. It was but eternal torture—which existed only in the clouded imagination of the believer—that was escaped by the forgiveness of sins;

[1] See *ante*, Chap. VIII.

and we may perhaps go so far as to suggest that the
dogmatist, having postulated an eternal hell as the
monstrous result of transient errors, felt compelled to
provide a way of escape from an incredible and unjust
fate, and therefore further postulated an incredible and
unjust forgiveness. Schemes that are elaborated by
human speculation, without regard to the facts of life,
are apt to land the speculator in thought-morasses,
whence he can only extricate himself by blundering
through the mire in an opposite direction. A superfluous eternal hell was balanced by a superfluous forgiveness, and thus the uneven scales of justice were
again rendered level. Leaving these aberrations of the
unenlightened, let us return into the realm of fact and
right reason.

When a man has committed an evil action he has
attached himself to a sorrow, for sorrow is ever the
plant that springs from the seed of sin. It may be
said, even more accurately, that sin and sorrow are but
the two sides of one act, not two separate events. As
every object has two sides, one of which is behind, out
of sight, when the other is in front, in sight, so every
act has two sides, which cannot both be seen
in the physical world. In other words, good and
happiness, evil and sorrow, are seen as the two sides of
the same thing. This is what is called karma—a con-
venient and now widely-used term, originally Samskrit,
expressing this connection or identity, literally meaning
" action "—and the suffering is therefore called the
karmic result of the wrong. The result, the " other

side ", may not follow immediately, may not even accrue during the present incarnation but sooner or later it will appear and clasp the sinner with its arms of pain.

Now a result in the physical world, an effect experienced through our physical consciousness, is the final outcome of a cause set going in the past; it is the ripened fruit; in it a particular force becomes manifest and exhausts itself. That force has been working outwards, and its effects are already over in the mind ere it appears in the body. Its bodily manifestation, its appearance, in the physical world, is the sign of the completion of its course.[1] If at such a moment the sinner, having exhausted the karma of his sin, comes into contact with a sage who can see the past and the present, the invisible and the visible, such a sage may discern the ending of the particular karma, and, the sentence being completed, may declare the captive free. Such an instance seems to be given in the story of the man sick of the palsy, already alluded to, a case typical of many. A physical ailment is the last expression of a past ill-doing; the mental and moral outworking is completed, and the sufferer is brought—by the agency of some angel, as an administrator of the law—into the presence of One able to relieve physical disease by the exertion of a higher energy. First, the Initiate declares that the man's sins are forgiven, and then justifies his insight by the authoritative word, " Arise, take up thy bed, and go unto thine

[1] This is the cause of the sweetness and patience often noticed in the sick who are of very pure nature. They have learned the lesson of suffering, and they do not make fresh evil karma by impatience under the result of past bad karma, then exhausting itself.

house." Had no such enlightened One been there, the disease would have passed away under the restoring touch of nature, under a force applied by the invisible angelic Intelligences, who carry out in this world the workings of karmic law; when a greater One is acting, this force is of more swiftly compelling power, and the physical vibrations are at once attuned to the harmony that is health.

All such forgiveness of sins may be termed declaratory; the karma is exhausted, and a "knower of karma" declares the fact. The assurance brings a relief to the mind, that is akin to the relief experienced by a prisoner when the order for his release is given, that order being as much a part of the law as the original sentence; but the relief of the man who thus learns of the exhaustion of an evil karma is keener, because he cannot himself tell the term of its action.

It is noticeable that these declarations of forgiveness are constantly coupled with the statement that the sufferer showed "faith", and that without this nothing could be done; *i.e.*, the real agent in the ending of this karma is the sinner himself. In the case of the " woman that was a sinner ", the two declarations are coupled: " Thy sins are forgiven. . . . Thy faith hath saved thee; go in peace." [1] This " faith " is the upwelling in man of his own divine essence, seeking the divine ocean of like essence, and when this breaks through the lower nature that holds it in—as the water-spring breaks through the encumbering earth-clods—the power thus

[1] St. Luke, vii, 48, 40.

liberated works on the whole nature, bringing it into harmony with itself. The man only becomes conscious of this as the karmic crust of evil is broken up by its force, and that glad consciousness of a power within himself, hitherto unknown, asserting itself as soon as the evil karma is exhausted, is a large factor in the joy, relief, and new strength that follow on the feeling that sin is " forgiven ", that its results are past.

And this brings us to the heart of the subject—the changes that go on in a man's inner nature, unrecognized by that part of his consciousness which works within the limits of his brain, until they suddenly assert themselves within those limits, coming apparently from nowhere, bursting forth "from the blue", pouring from an unknown source. What wonder that a man, bewildered by their downrush—knowing nothing of the mysteries of his own nature, nothing of "the inner God " that is verily himself—imagines that to be from without which is really from within, and, unconscious of his own Divinity, thinks only of Divinities in the world external to himself. And this misconception is the more easy, because the final touch, the vibration that breaks the imprisoning shell, is often the answer from the Divinity within another man, or within some superhuman being, responding to the insistent cry from the imprisoned Divinity within himself; he oft-times recognizes the brotherly aid, while not recognizing that he himself, the cry from his inner nature, called it forth.

As an explanation from one wiser than ourselves may make an intellectual difficulty clear to our mind, though it is our own mind that, thus aided, grasps the solution; as an encouraging word from one purer than ourselves may nerve us to a moral effort that we should have thought beyond our power, though it is our own strength that makes it; so may a loftier Spirit than our own, one more conscious of its Divinity, aid us to put forth our own divine energy, though it is that very putting forth that lifts us to a higher plane. We are all bound by ties of brotherly help to those above us as to those below us, and why should we, who so constantly find ourselves able to help in their development souls less advanced than ourselves, hesitate to admit that we can receive similar help from those far above us, and that our progress may be rendered much swifter by their aid?

Now among the changes that go on in a man's inner nature, unknown to his lower consciousness, are those that have to do with the putting forth of his will. The Ego, glancing backward over his past, balancing up its results, suffering under its mistakes, determines on a change of attitude, on a change of activity. While his lower vehicle is still under his former impulse, plunging along lines of action that bring sharp collisions with the law, the Ego determines on an opposite course of conduct. Hitherto he has turned his face longingly to the animal, the pleasures of the lower world have held him fast enchained. Now he turns his face to the true goal of evolution, and determines to work for loftier joys. He sees that the whole world is evolving, and that if he sets himself against that mighty current it dashes

15

him aside, bruising him sorely in the process; that if he sets himself with it, it will bear him onwards on its bosom and land him in the desired haven.

He then resolves to change his life, he turns determinedly on his steps, he faces the other way. The first result of the effort to turn his lower nature into the changed course is much distress and disturbance. The habits formed under the impacts of the old views resist stubbornly the impulses flowing from the new, and a bitter conflict arises. Gradually the consciousness working in the brain accepts the decision made on higher planes, and then " becomes conscious of sin " by this very recognition of the law. The sense of error deepens, remorse preys on the mind; spasmodic efforts are made towards improvement, and, frustrated by old habits, repeatedly fail, till the man, overwhelmed by grief for the past, despair of the present, is plunged into hopeless gloom. At last, the ever-increasing suffering wrings from the Ego a cry for help, answered from the inner depths of his own nature, from the God within as well as around him, the Life of his life. He turns from the lower nature that is thwarting him to the higher which is his innermost being, from the separated self that tortures him to the One Self that is the Heart of all.

But this change of front means that he turns his face from the darkness, that he turns his face to the light. The light was always there, but his back was towards it; now he sees the sun, and its radiance cheers his eyes, and overfloods his being with delight. His heart was closed; it is now flung open, and the ocean of life flows in, in full tide, suffusing him with joy. Wave after wave of new life uplifts him, and the gladness of the dawn surrounds him. He sees his past as past, because his will is set to follow a higher path, and he recks little of the suffering that the past may bequeath to him, since he knows he will not hand on such bitter legacy from his present. This sense of peace, of joy, of freedom, is the feeling spoken of as the result of the forgiveness of sins. The obstacles set up by the lower nature between the God within and the God without are swept away, and that nature scarce recognizes that the change is in itself and not in the Oversoul. As a child, having thrust away the mother's guiding hand and hidden its face against the wall, may fancy itself alone and forgotten, until, turning with a cry, it finds around it the protecting mother-arms that were never but a handsbreadth away, so does man in his wilfulness push away the shielding arms of the divine Mother of the worlds, only to find, when he turns back his face, that he has never been outside their protecting shelter, and that wherever he may wander that guarding love is round him still.

The key to this change in the man, that brings about "forgiveness", is given in the verse of the *Bhagavad Gita* already partly quoted: " Even if the most sinful worship me, with undivided heart, he too must be accounted righteous, *for he hath rightly resolved.*" On that right resolution follows the inevitable result: " Speedily he becometh dutiful and goeth to peace." [1] The essence of sin lies in setting the will of the part against the will

[1] *Loc. cit.*, ix, 31.

of the whole, the human against the Divine. When this is changed, when the Ego puts his separate will into union with the will that works for evolution, then, in the world where to will is to do, in the world where effects are seen as present in causes, the man is " accounted righteous "; the effects on the lower planes must inevitably follow; " speedily he becometh dutiful " in action, having already become dutiful in will. Here we judge by actions, the dead leaves of the past; there they judge by wills, the germinating seeds of the future. Hence the Christ ever says to men in the lower world: " Judge not." [1]

Even after the new direction has been definitely followed, and has become the normal habit of the life, there come times of failure, alluded to in the *Pistis Sophia*, when Jesus is asked whether a man may be again admitted to the Mysteries, after he has fallen away, if he again repents. The answer of Jesus is in the affirmative, but he states that a time comes when re-admission is beyond the power of any save of the highest Mystery, who pardons ever. " Amen, amen, I say unto you, whosoever shall receive the mysteries of the first mystery, and then shall turn back and transgress twelve times (even), and then should again repent twelve times, offering prayer in the mystery of the first mystery, he shall be forgiven. But if he should transgress after twelve times, should he turn back and transgress, it shall not be remitted unto him for ever, so that he may turn again unto his mystery, whatever it be. For him there

[1] St. Matt., vii, 1.

is no means of repentance unless he have received the mysteries of that ineffable, which hath compassion at all times and remitteth sins for ever and ever." [1] These restorations after failure, in which "sin is remitted", meet us in human life, especially in the higher phases of evolution. A man is offered an opportunity, which, taken, would open to him new possibilities of growth. He fails to grasp it, and falls away from the position he had gained that made the further opportunity possible. For him, for the time, further progress is blocked; he must turn all his efforts wearily to retread the ground he had already trodden, and to regain and make sure his footing on the place from which he had slipped. Only when this is accomplished will he hear the gentle Voice that tells him that the past is outworn, the weakness turned to strength, and that the gateway is again open for his passage. Here again the "forgiveness" is but the declaration by a proper authority of the true state of affairs, the opening of the gate to the competent, its closure to the incompetent. Where there had been failure, with its accompanying suffering, this declaration would be felt as a "baptism for the remission of sins", readmitting the aspirant to a privilege lost by his own act; this would certainly give rise to feelings of joy and peace, to a relief from the burden of sorrow, to a feeling that the clog of the past had at last fallen from the feet.

Remains one truth that should never be forgotten; that we are living in an ocean of light, of love, of bliss, that surrounds us at all times, the Life of God. As the

[1] *Loc. cit.*, bk. ii, § 305.

sun floods the earth with his radiance, so does that Life enlighten all, only that Sun of the world never sets to any part of it. We shut this light out of our consciousness by our selfishness, our heartlessness, our impurity, our intolerance, but it shines on us ever the same, bathing us on every side, pressing against our self-built walls with gentle, strong persistence. When the soul throws down these excluding walls, the light flows in, and the soul finds itself flooded with sunshine, breathing the blissful air of heaven. " For the Son of man is in heaven," though he know it not, and its breezes fan his brow if he bares it to their breaths. God ever respects man's individuality, and will not enter his consciousness until that consciousness opens to give welcome; " Behold I stand at the door and knock " [1] is the attitude of every spiritual Intelligence towards the evolving human soul; not in lack of sympathy is rooted that waiting for the open door, but in deepest wisdom.

Man is not to be compelled; he is to be free. He is not a slave, but a God in the making, and the growth cannot be forced, but must be willed from within. Only when the will consents, as Giordano Bruno teaches, will God influence man, though He be " everywhere present, and ready to come to the aid of whosoever turns to Him through the act of the intelligence, and who unreservedly presents himself with the affection of the will." [2] " The divine potency which is all in all does

[1] Rev., iii, 20.

[2] Giordano Bruno, trans. by L. Williams. *The Heroic Enthusiasts*, vol. i, p. 133.

not proffer or withhold, except through assimilation or rejection by oneself." [1] " It is taken in quickly, as the solar light, without hesitation, and makes itself present to whoever turns himself to it and opens himself to it . . . the windows are opened, but the sun enters in a moment, so does it happen similarly in this case." [2]

The sense of " forgiveness ", then, is the feeling which fills the heart with joy when the will is tuned to harmony with the Divine, when, the soul having opened its windows, the sunshine of love and light and bliss pours in, when the part feels its oneness with the whole, and the One Life thrills each vein.   This is the noble truth that gives vitality to even the crudest presentation of the " forgiveness of sins ", and that makes it often, despite its intellectual incompleteness, an inspirer to pure and spiritual living.   And this is the truth, as seen in the Lesser Mysteries.

[1] *Ibid.*, vol. ii, pp. 27, 28.
[2] *Ibid.*, pp. 102, 103.

CHAPTER XII

SACRAMENTS

IN all religions there exist certain ceremonials, or rites, which are regarded as of vital importance by the believers in the religion, and which are held to confer certain benefits on those taking part in them. The word Sacrament, or some equivalent term, has been applied to these ceremonials, and they all have the same character. Little exact exposition has been given as to their nature and meaning, but this is another of the subjects explained of old in the Lesser Mysteries.

The peculiar characteristic of a sacrament resides in two of its properties. First, there is the exoteric ceremony, which is a pictorial allegory, a representation of something by actions and materials—not a verbal allegory, a teaching given in words, conveying a truth; but an acted representation, certain definite material things used in a particular way. The object in choosing these materials, and aimed at in the ceremonies by which their manipulation is accompanied, is to represent, as in a picture, some truth which it is desired to impress upon the minds of the people present. That is the first and obvious property of a sacrament, differentiating it from other forms of worship and meditation. It appeals to those who without this imagery would fail to catch a subtle truth, and shows to them in a vivid and graphic form the truth which otherwise would escape them. Every sacrament, when it is studied, should be taken first from this standpoint that it is a pictorial allegory; the essential things to be studied will therefore be: the material objects which enter into the allegory, the method in which they are employed, and the meaning which the whole is intended to convey.

The second characteristic property of a sacrament belongs to the facts of the invisible worlds, and is studied by occult science. The person who officiates in the sacrament should possess this knowledge, as much, though not all, of the operative power of the sacrament depends on the knowledge of the officiator. A sacrament links the material world with the subtle and invisible regions to which that world is related; it is a link between the visible and the invisible. And it is not only a link between this world and other worlds, but it is also a method by which the energies of the invisible world are transmuted into action in the physical; an actual method of changing energies of one kind into energies of another, as literally as in the galvanic cell chemical energies are changed into electrical. The essence of all energies is one and the same, whether in the visible or invisible worlds; but the energies differ according to the grades of matter through which they manifest. A sacrament serves as a kind of crucible in which spiritual alchemy takes place. An energy placed in this crucible and subjected to certain manipulations comes forth different in expression. Thus an energy of a subtle kind, belonging to one of the higher regions of the universe, may be brought into direct relation with people living in the physical world, and may be made to affect them in the physical world as well as in its own realm; the sacrament forms the last bridge from the invisible to the visible, and enables the energies to be directly applied to those who fulfil the necessary conditions and who take part in the sacrament.

The sacraments of the Christian Church lost much of their dignity and of the recognition of their occult power among those who separated from the Roman Catholic Church at the time of the " Reformation ". The previous separation between the East and the West, leaving the Greek Orthodox Church on the one side and the Roman Church on the other, in no way affected belief in the sacraments. They remained in both great communities as the recognized links between the seen and the unseen, and sanctified the life of the believer from cradle to grave. The seven sacraments of Christianity cover the whole of life, from the welcome of baptism to the farewell of extreme unction. They were established by occultists, by men who knew the invisible worlds; and the materials used, the words spoken, the signs made, were all deliberately chosen and arranged with a view to bringing about certain results.

At the time of the Reformation, the seceding churches, which threw off the yoke of Rome, were not led by occultists, but by ordinary men of the world, some good and some bad, but all profoundly ignorant of the facts of the invisible worlds, and conscious only of the outer shell of Christianity, its literal dogmas and exoteric worship. The consequence of this was that the sacraments lost their supreme place in Christian worship, and in most Protestant communities were reduced to two, baptism and the Eucharist.

The sacramental nature of the others was not explicitly denied in the most important of the seceding Churches, but the two were set apart from the five, as of universal obligation, of which every member of the Church must partake in order to be recognized as a full member.

The general definition of a sacrament is given quite accurately, save for the superfluous words, "ordained by Christ Himself", in the Catechism of the Church of England, and even these words might be retained if the mystic meaning be given to the word "Christ." A Sacrament is there said to be: "An outward and visible sign of an inward and spiritual grace given unto us, ordained by Christ Himself, as a means whereby we receive the same and a pledge to assure us thereof."

In this definition we find laid down the two distinguishing characteristics of a Sacrament as given above. The "outward and visible sign" is the pictorial allegory, and the phrase, the "means whereby we receive the" "inward and spiritual grace" covers the second property. This last phrase should be carefully noted by those members of Protestant churches who regard sacraments as mere external forms and outer ceremonies. For it distinctly alleges that the sacrament is really a means whereby the grace is conveyed, and thus implies that without it the grace does not pass in the same fashion from the spiritual to the physical world. It is the distinct recognition of a sacrament in its second aspect, as a means whereby spiritual powers are brought into activity on earth.

In order to understand a sacrament, it is necessary that we should definitely recognize the existence of an occult, or hidden, side of Nature; this is spoken of as the life-side of Nature, the consciousness-side, more accurately the mind in Nature. Underlying all sacramental action there is the belief that the invisible world exercises a potent influence over the visible, and to understand a sacrament we must understand something of the invisible Intelligences who administer Nature. We have seen in studying the doctrine of the Trinity that Spirit is manifested as the triple Self, and that as the field for His manifestation there is matter, the form-side of Nature, often regarded, and rightly, as Nature herself. We have to study both these aspects, the side of life and that of form, in order to understand a Sacrament.

Stretching between the Trinity and humanity are many grades and hierarchies of invisible beings; the highest of these are the seven Spirits of God, the seven Fires, or Flames, that are before the throne of God.[1] Each of these stands at the head of a vast host of Intelligences, all of whom share His nature and act under His direction; these are themselves graded, and are the

[1] Rev., iv, 5.

Thrones, Powers, Princes, Dominations, Archangels, Angels, of whom mention is found in the writings of the Christian Fathers, who were versed in the Mysteries. Thus there are seven great hosts of these Beings, and they represent in their intelligence the divine Mind in nature. They are found in all regions, and they ensoul the energies of Nature. From the standpoint of Occultism there is no dead force and no dead matter. Force and matter alike are living and active, and an energy or a group of energies is the veil of an Intelligence, of a Consciousness, who has that energy as his outer expression, and the matter in which that energy moves yields a form which he guides or ensouls. Unless a man can thus look at Nature all esoteric teaching must remain for him a sealed book. Without these angelic lives, these countless invisible intelligences, these consciousnesses which ensoul the force and matter [1] which is Nature, Nature herself would not only remain unintelligible, but she would be out of relation alike to the divine Life that moves within and around her, and to the human lives that are developing in her midst. These innumerable angels link the worlds together; they are themselves evolving while helping the evolution of beings lower than themselves, and a new light is shed on evolution when we see that men form grades in these hierarchies of intelligent beings. These angels are the " sons of God " of an earlier birth than

---

[1] The phrase " force and matter " is used as it is so well-known in science. But force is one of the properties of matter, the one mentioned as Motion. See *Ante*, p. 180.

ours, who " shouted for joy " [1] when the foundations of the earth were laid amid the choiring of the morning stars.

Other beings are below us in evolution—animals, plants, minerals, and elemental lives—as the Angels are above us; and as we thus study, a conception dawns upon us of a vast Wheel of Life, of numberless existences, interrelated and necessary each to each, man as a living Intelligence, as a self-conscious being, having his own place in this Wheel. The Wheel is ever turning by the divine Will and the living Intelligences who form it learn to co-operate with that Will, and if in the action of those Intelligences there is any break or gap due to neglect or opposition, then the Wheel drags, turning slowly, and the chariot of the evolution of the worlds goes but heavily upon its way.

These numberless lives, above and below man, come into touch with human consciousness in very definite ways, and among these ways are sounds and colours. Each sound has a form in the invisible world, and combinations of sounds create complicated shapes.[2] In the subtle matter of those worlds all sounds are accompanied by colours, so that they give rise to many-hued shapes, in many cases exceedingly beautiful. The vibrations set up in the visible world when a note is sounded set up vibrations in the worlds invisible, each

[1] Job, xxxviii, 7.

[2] See on forms created by musical notes any scientific book on Sound, and also Mrs. Watts-Hughes' illustrated book on *Voice Figures*.

one with its own specific character, and capable of producing certain effects. In communicating with the sub-human Intelligences connected with the lower invisible world and with the physical, and in controlling and directing these, sounds must be used fitted to bring about the desired results, as language made up of definite sounds is used here. And in communicating with the higher Intelligences certain sounds are useful, to create a harmonious atmosphere, suitable for their activities, and to make our own subtle bodies receptive of their influences.

This effect on the subtle bodies is a most important part of the occult use of sounds. These bodies, like the physical, are in constant vibratory motion, the vibrations changing with every thought or desire. These changing irregular vibrations offer an obstacle to any fresh vibration coming from outside, and, in order to render the bodies susceptible to the higher influences, sounds are used which reduce the irregular vibrations to a steady rhythm, like in its nature to the rhythm of the Intelligence sought to be reached. The object of all often-repeated sentences is to effect this, as a musician sounds the same note over and over again, until all the instruments are in tune. The subtle bodies must be tuned to the note of the Being sought, if his influence is to find free way through the nature of the worshipper, and this was ever done of old by the use of sounds. Hence, music has ever formed an integral part of worship and certain definite cadences have been preserved with the care handed on from age to age.

In every religion there exist sounds of a peculiar character, called "words of power", consisting of sentences in a particular language chanted in a particular way; each religion possesses a stock of such sentences, special successions of sounds, now very generally called "mantras", that being the name given to them in the East, where the science of mantras has been much studied and elaborated. It is not necessary that a mantra—a succession of sounds arranged in a particular manner to bring about a definite result— should be in any one particular language. Any language can be used for the purpose, though some are more suitable than others, provided that the person who makes the mantra possesses the requisite occult knowledge. There are hundreds of mantras in the Samskrit tongue, made by occultists of the past, who were familiar with the laws of the invisible worlds. These have been handed down from generation to generation, definite words in a definite order chanted in a definite way. The effect of the chanting is to create vibrations, hence forms, in the physical and superphysical worlds, and according to the knowledge and purity of the singer will be the worlds his song is able to affect. If his knowledge be wide and deep, if his will be strong and his heart pure, there is scarcely any limit to the powers he may exercise in using some of these ancient mantras.

As said, it is not necessary that any one particular language should be used. They may be in Samskrit or in any one of the languages of the world, in which men of knowledge have put them together.

This is the reason why, in the Roman Catholic Church, the Latin language, is used in important acts of worship. It is not used as a dead language here, a tongue " not understood of the people ", but as a living force in the invisible worlds. It is not used to hide knowledge from the people, but in order that certain vibrations may be set up in the invisible worlds which cannot be set up in the ordinary languages of Europe, unless a great occultist should compose in them the necessary successions of sounds. To translate a mantra is to change it from a " Word of Power " into an ordinary sentence; the sounds being changed, other sound-forms are created.

Some of the arrangements of Latin words, with the music wedded to them in Christian worship, cause the most marked effects in the supra-physical worlds, and any one who is at all sensitive will be conscious of peculiar effects caused by the chanting of some of the most sacred sentences, especially in the Mass. Vibratory effects may be felt by any one who will sit quiet and receptive as some of these sentences are uttered by priest or choristers. And at the same time effects are caused in the higher worlds directly affecting the subtle bodies of the worshippers in the way above described, and also appealing to the Intelligences in those worlds with a meaning as definite as the words addressed by one person to another on the physical plane, whether as prayer or, in some cases, as command. The sounds, causing active flashing forms, rise through the worlds, affecting the consciousness of the Intelligences residing in them,

16

and bringing some of them to render the definite services required by those who are taking part in the church office.

Such mantras form an essential part of every sacrament.

The next essential part of the sacrament, in its outward and visible form, are certain gestures. These are called signs, or seals, or sigils—the three words meaning the same thing in a sacrament. Each sign has its own particular meaning, and marks the direction imposed on the invisible forces with which the celebrant is dealing, whether those forces be his own or poured through him. In any case, they are needed to bring about the desired result, and they are an essential portion of the sacramental rite. Such a sign is called a " sign of power ", as the mantra is a " word of power."

It is interesting to read in occult works of the past references to these facts, true then as now, true now as then. In the Egyptian *Book of the Dead* is described the *post-mortem* journey of the soul, and we read how he is stopped and challenged at various stages of that journey. He is stopped and challenged by the Guardians of the Gate of each successive world, and the soul cannot pass through the Gate and go on his way unless he knows two things: he must pronounce a word, the word of power: he must make a sign, the sign of power. When that word is spoken, when that sign is given, the bars of the gate fall down, and the guardians stand aside to let the soul pass through. A similar account is given in the great mystic Christian Gospel, the *Pistis*

Sophia, before mentioned.[1] Here the passage through the world is not of a soul set free from the body by death, but of one who has voluntarily left it in the course of initiation. There are greater powers, the powers of Nature, that bar his way, and till the initiate gives the word and the sign, they will not allow him to pass through the portals of their realms. This double knowledge, then, was necessary—to speak the word of power, to make the sign of power. Without these progress was blocked, and without these a sacrament is no sacrament.

Further, in all sacraments some physical material is used, or should be used.[2] This is ever a symbol of that which is to be gained by the sacrament, and points to the nature of the " inward and spiritual grace " received through it. This is also the material means of conveying the grace, not symbolically, but actually, and a subtle change in this material adapts it for high ends.

Now a physical object consists of the solid, liquid, and gaseous particles into which a chemist would resolve it by analysis, and further of ether, which interpenetrates the grosser stuffs. In this ether play the magnetic energies. It is further connected with counterparts of subtle matter, in which play energies subtler than the magnetic, but like them in nature and more powerful.

When such an object is magnetized a change is effected in the ethereal portion, the wave-motions are altered

[1] See *Ante*, pp. 96 and 208.

[2] In the Sacrament of Penance the ashes are now usually omitted, except on special occasions, but none the less they form part of the rite.

and systematized, and made to follow the wave-motions of the ether of the magnetizer; it thus comes to share his nature, and the denser particles of the object, played on by the ether, slowly change their rate of vibration. If the magnetizer has the power of affecting the subtler counterparts also he makes them similarly vibrate in assonance with his own.

This is the secret of magnetic cures; the irregular vibrations of the diseased person are so worked on as to accord with the regular vibrations of the healthy operator, as definitely as an irregularly swinging object may be made to swing regularly by repeated and timed blows. A doctor will magnetize water and cure his patient therewith. He will magnetize a cloth, and the cloth laid on the seat of pain, will heal. He will use a powerful magnet, or a current from a galvanic cell, and restore energy to a nerve. In all cases the ether is thrown into motion, and by this the denser physical particles are affected.

A similar result accrues when the materials used in a sacrament are acted on by the word of power and the sign of power. Magnetic changes are caused in the ether of the physical substance, and the subtle counterparts are affected according to the knowledge, purity, and devotion of the celebrant who magnetizes—or, in the religious term, consecrates—it. Further, the word and the sign of power summon to the celebration the angels specially concerned with the materials used and the nature of the act performed, and they lend their powerful aid, pouring their own magnetic energies into the subtle counterparts, and even into the physical ether, thus reinforcing the energies of the celebrant. No one who knows anything of the powers of magnetism can doubt the possibility of the changes in material objects thus indicated. Those who are able to sense the higher forms of magnetism know very well that consecrated objects vary much in their power, and that the magnetic difference is due to the varying knowledge, purity, and spirituality of the priest who consecrates them.

We thus see that the outer part of the sacrament is of very great importance. Real changes are made in the materials used. They are made the vehicles of energies higher than those which naturally belong to them; persons approaching them, touching them, will have their own etheric and subtle bodies affected by their potent magnetism, and will be brought into a condition very receptive of higher influences, being tuned into accord with the lofty Beings connected with the word and the sign used in consecration; beings belonging to the invisible world will be present during the sacramental rite, pouring out their benign and gracious influence; and thus all who are worthy participants in the ceremony—sufficiently pure and devoted to be tuned by the vibrations caused—will find their emotions purified and stimulated, their spirituality quickened, and their hearts filled with peace, by coming into such close touch with the unseen realities.

CHAPTER XIII

SACRAMENTS (*Continued*)

WE have now to apply these general principles to concrete examples, and to see how they explain and justify the sacramental rites found in all religions.

It will be sufficient if we take as examples three out of the seven sacraments used in the Church Catholic. Two are recognized as obligatory by all Christians, although extreme Protestants deprive them of their sacramental character, giving them a declaratory and remembrance value only instead of a sacramental; yet even among them the heart of true devotion wins something of the sacramental blessing the head denies. The third is not recognized as even nominally a sacrament by Protestant churches, though it shows the essential signs of a sacrament, as given in the definition in the Catechism of the Church of England already quoted.[1] The first is that of baptism; the second that of the Eucharist; the third that of marriage. The putting of marriage out of the rank of a sacrament has much degraded its lofty ideal, and has led to much of that loosening of its tie that thinking men deplore.

The sacrament of baptism is found in all religions, not only at the entrance into earth-life but more generally

[1] See *Ante*, p. 225.

as a ceremony of purification. The ceremony which admits the new-born—or adult—incomer into a religion has a sprinkling with water as an essential part of the rite, and this was as universal in ancient days as it is now. The Rev. Dr. Giles remarks: " The idea of using water as emblematic of spiritual washing is too obvious to allow surprise at the antiquity of this rite. Dr. Hyde, in his treatise on the *Religion of the Ancient Persians*, xxxiv, 406, tells us that it prevailed among that people. ' They do not use circumcision for their children, but only baptism, or washing for the purification of the soul. They bring the child to the priest into the church, and place him in front of the sun and fire, which ceremony being completed, they look upon him as more sacred than before. Lord says that they bring the water for this purpose in bark of the Holm-tree; that tree is in truth the Haum of the Magi, of which we spoke before on another occasion. Sometimes also it is otherwise done by immersing him in a large vessel of water, as Tavernier tells us. After such washing, or baptism, the priest imposes on the child the name given by the parents '." [1] A few weeks after the birth of a Hindu child a ceremony is performed, a part of which consists in sprinkling the child with water—such sprinkling entering into all Hindu worship. Williamson gives authorities for the practice of Baptism in Egypt, Persia, Tibet, Mongolia, Mexico, Peru, Greece, Rome, Scandinavia, and among the Druids. [2] Some of the prayers

[1] *Christian Records*, p. 129.
[2] *The Great Law*, pp. 161-166.

quoted are very fine: " I pray that this celestial water, blue and light blue, may enter into thy body and there live. I pray that it may destroy in thee, and put away from thee, all the things evil and adverse that were given to thee before the beginning of the world." " O child! receive the water of the Lord of the world who is our life; it is to wash and to purify; may these drops remove the sin which was given to thee before the creation of the world, since all of us are under its power."

Tertullian mentions the very general use of baptism among non-Christian nations in a passage already quoted,[1] and others of the Fathers refer to it.

In most religious communities a minor form of baptism accompanies all religious ceremonies, water being used as symbol of purification, and the idea being that no man should enter upon worship until he has purified his heart and conscience, the outer washing symbolizing the inner lustration. In the Greek and Roman Churches a small receptacle for holy water is placed near every door, and every incoming worshipper touches it, making with it on himself the sign of the cross ere he goes onward towards the altar. On this Robert Taylor remarks: " The baptismal fonts in our Protestant churches, and we need hardly say more especially the little cisterns at the entrance of our Catholic chapels, are not imitations, but an unbroken and never interrupted, continuation of the same *aqua minaria*, or *amula*, which the learned Montfaucon, in his *Antiquities*, shows to have been vases of holy water, which were placed by the

[1] See *ante*, p. 105.

heathens at the entrance of their temples, to sprinkle themselves with upon entering those sacred edifices." [1]

Whether in the baptism of initial reception into the Church, or in these minor lustrations, water is the material agent employed, the great cleansing fluid in Nature, and therefore the best symbol for purification. Over this water a mantra is pronounced, in the English ritual represented by the prayer, " Sanctify this water to the mystical washing away of sin", concluding with the formula, " In the name of the Father, and of the Son, and of the Holy Ghost. Amen." This is the word of power, and it is accompanied by the sign of power, the sign of the cross made over the surface of the water.

The word and the sign give to the water, as before explained, a property it previously had not, and it is rightly named " holy water ". The dark powers will not approach it; sprinkled on the body it gives a sense of peace, and conveys new spiritual life. When a child is baptised, the spiritual energy given to the water by the word and the sign reinforces the spiritual life in the child, and then the word of power is again spoken, this time over the child, and the sign is traced on his forehead, and in his subtle bodies the vibrations are felt, and the summons to guard the life thus sanctified goes forth through the invisible world; for this sign is at once purifying and protective—purifying by the life that is poured forth through it, protective by the vibrations it sets up in the subtle bodies. Those vibrations form a guardian wall against the attacks of hostile influences in

[1] *Diegesis*, p. 219.

the invisible worlds, and every time that holy water is touched, the word pronounced, and the sign made, the energy is renewed, the vibrations are reinforced, both being recognized as potent in the invisible worlds, and bringing aid to the operator.

In the early Church, baptism was preceded by a very careful preparation, those admitted to the Church being mostly converts from surrounding faiths. A convert passed through three definite stages of instruction, remaining in each grade till he had mastered its teachings, and he was then admitted to the Church by baptism. Only after that was he taught the Creed, which was not committed to writing, nor ever repeated in the presence of an unbeliever; it thus served as a sign of recognition, and a proof of the position of the man who was able to recite it, showing that he was a baptized member of the Church. How truly in those days the grace conveyed by baptism was believed in is shown by the custom of death-bed baptism that grew up. Believing in the reality of baptism, men and women of the world, unwilling to resign its pleasures or to keep their lives pure from stain, would put off the rite of baptism until death's hand was upon them, so that they might benefit by the sacramental grace, and pass through death's portal pure and clean, full of spiritual energy. Against that abuse some of the great Fathers of the Church struggle, and struggle effectively. There is a quaint story told by one of them, I think by St. Athanasius, who was a man of caustic wit, not averse to the use of humour in the attempt to make his hearers understand at times the folly or perversity of their behaviour. He told his congregation that he had had a vision, and had gone up to the gateway of heaven where St. Peter stood as Warder. No pleased smile had he for the visitant, but a frown of stern displeasure. " Athanasius," said he, " why are you continually sending me these empty bags, carefully sealed up, with nothing inside? " It was one of the piercing sayings we meet with in Christian antiquity, when these things were real to Christian men, and not mere forms, as they too often are today.

The custom of infant baptism gradually grew up in the Church, and hence the instruction which in the early days preceded baptism came to be the preparation for confirmation, when the awakened mind and intelligence take up and reaffirm the baptismal promises. The reception of the infant into the Church is seen to be rightly done, when man's life is recognized as being lived in the three worlds, and when the Spirit and Soul who have come to inhabit the new-born body are known to be not unconscious and unintelligent, but conscious, intelligent, and potent in the invisible worlds. It is right and just that the " Hidden Man of the heart " [1] should be welcomed to the new stage of his pilgrimage, and that the most helpful influences should be brought to bear upon the vehicle in which he is to dwell, and which he has to mould to his service. If the eyes of men were opened, as were of old those of the servant of Elisha, they would still see the horses and chariots of fire gathered round the mountain where is the prophet of the Lord. [2]

[1] 1 Pet., iii, 4.   [2] II Kings, vi, 17.

We come to the second of the sacraments selected for study, that of the sacrifice of the Eucharist, a symbol of the eternal sacrifice already explained, the daily sacrifice of the Church Catholic throughout the world imaging that eternal sacrifice by which the worlds were made, and by which they are evermore sustained. It is to be daily offered, as its archetype is perpetually existent, and men in that act take part in the working of the Law of Sacrifice, identify themselves with it, recognize its binding nature, and voluntarily associate themselves with it in its working in the worlds; in such identification, to partake of the material part of the sacrament is necessary, if the identification is to be complete, but many of the benefits may be shared, and the influence going forth to the worlds may be increased, by devout worshippers, who associate themselves mentally, but not physically, with the act.

This great function of Christian worship loses its force and meaning when it is regarded as nothing more than a mere commemoration of a past sacrifice, as a pictorial allegory without a deep ensouling truth, as a breaking of bread and a pouring out of wine without a sharing in the eternal sacrifice. So to see it is to make it a mere shell, a dead picture instead of a living reality. " The cup of blessing which we bless, is it not the communion (the communication of, the sharing in) of the blood of Christ?" asks the apostle. " The bread which we break, is it not the communion of the body of Christ?" [1] And he goes on to point out that all who

[1] I Cor., x, 16.

eat of a sacrifice become partakers of a common nature, and are joined into a single body, which is united to, shares the nature of, that Being who is present in the sacrifice. A fact of the invisible world is here concerned, and he speaks with the authority of knowledge. Invisible beings pour of their essence into the materials used in any sacramental rite, and those who partake of those materials—which become assimilated in the body and enter into its ingredients—are thereby united to those whose essence is in it, and they all share a common nature. This is true when we take even ordinary food from the hand of another—part of his nature, his vital magnetism, mingles with our own; how much more true then when the food has been solemnly and purposely impregnated with higher magnetisms, which affect the subtle bodies as well as the physical! If we would understand the meaning and use of the Eucharist we must realize these facts of the invisible worlds, and we must see in it a link between the earthly and the heavenly, as well as an act of the universal worship, a co-operation, an association, with the Law of Sacrifice, else it loses the greater part of its significance.

The employment of bread and wine as the materials for this sacrament—like the use of water in the sacrament of baptism—is of very ancient and general usage. The Persians offered bread and wine to Mithra, and similar offerings were made in Tibet and Tartary. Jeremiah speaks of the cakes and the drink offered to the Queen of Heaven by the Jews in Egypt, they taking part in the Egyptian worship.[1] In Genesis we read that Melchisedek, the King-Initiate, used bread and wine in the blessing of Abraham.[2] In the various Greek Mysteries bread and wine were used, and Williamson mentions their use also among the Mexicans, Peruvians, and Druids.[3]

The bread stands as the general symbol for the food that builds up the body, and the wine as symbol of the blood, regarded as the life-fluid, "for the life of the flesh in the blood."[4] Hence members of a family are said to share the same blood, and to be of the blood of a person is to be of his kin. Hence, also, the old cere-monies of the "blood-covenant"; when a stranger was made one of a family or of a tribe, some drops of blood from a member were transfused into his veins, or he drank them—usually mingled with water—and was thenceforth considered as being a born member of the family or tribe, as being of its blood. Similarly, in the Eucharist, the worshippers partake of the bread, symbolizing the body, the nature, of the Christ, and of the wine symbolizing the blood, the life of the Christ, and become of His kin, one with Him.

The word of power is the formula "This is My Body", "This is My Blood." This it is which works the change which we shall consider in a moment, and transforms the materials into vehicles of spiritual energies. The sign of power is the hand extended over the

[1] Jer., xliv.   [2] Gen., xiv, 18, 19.
[3] *The Great Law*, pp. 177-181, 185.
[4] Lev., xvii, 11.

bread and the wine, and the sign of the cross should be made upon them, though this is not always done among Protestants. These are the outer essentials of the sacrament of the Eucharist.

It is important to understand the change which takes place in this sacrament, for it is more than the magnetization previously explained, though this also is wrought. We have here a special instance of a general law.

By the occultist, a visible thing is regarded as the last, the physical expression of an invisible truth. Everything is the physical expression of a thought. An object is but an idea externalized and densified. All the objects in the world are divine ideas expressed in physical matter. That being so, the reality of the object does not lie in the outer form but in the inner life, in the idea that has shaped and moulded the matter into an expression of itself. In the higher worlds, the matter being very subtle and plastic, shapes itself very swiftly to the idea, and changes form as the thought changes. As matter becomes denser, heavier, it changes form less readily, more slowly, until in the physical world, the changes are at their slowest in consequence of the resistance of the dense matter of which the physical world is composed. Let sufficient time be given, however, and even this heavy matter changes under the pressure of the ensouling idea, as may be seen by the graving on the face of the expressions of habitual thoughts and emotions.

This is the truth which underlies what is called the doctrine of Transubstantiation, so extraordinarily misunderstood by the ordinary Protestant. But such is the fate of occult truths when they are presented to the ignorant. The " substance " that is changed is the idea which makes a thing to be what it is; " bread " is not mere flour and water; the idea which governs the mixing, the manipulation of the flour and water, that is the " substance " which makes it " bread", and the flour and water are what are teachnically called the " accidents", the arrangements of matter that give form to the idea. With a different idea, or substance, flour and water would take a different form, as indeed they do when assimilated by the body. So also chemists have discovered that the same kind and the same number of chemical atoms may be arranged in different ways and thus become entirely different things in their properties, though the materials are unchanged; such " isomeric compounds " are among the most interesting of modern chemical discoveries; the arrangement of similar atoms under different ideas gives different bodies.

What, then, is this change of substance in the materials used in the Eucharist? The idea that makes the object has been changed; in their normal condition bread and wine are foodstuffs, expressive of the divine ideas of nutritive objects, objects fitted for the building up of bodies. The new idea is that of the Christ nature and life, fitted for the building up of the spiritual nature and life of man. That is the change of substance; the object remains unchanged in its " accidents", is physical material, but the subtle matter connected with it has changed under the pressure of the changed idea, and new properties are imparted by this change. They affect the subtle bodies of the participants, and attune them to the nature and life of the Christ. On the " worthiness " of the participant depends the extent to which he can be thus attuned.

The unworthy participant, subjected to the same process, is injuriously affected by it, for his nature, resisting the pressure, is bruised and rent by the forces to which it is unable to respond, as an object may be broken into pieces by vibrations which it is unable to reproduce.

The worthy partaker, then, becomes one with the sacrifice, with the Christ, and so becomes at-one with, also united to, the divine Life, which is the Father of the Christ. Inasmuch as the act of sacrifice on the side of form is the yielding up of the life it separates from others to be part of the common Life, the offering of the separated channel to be a channel of the one Life, so by that surrender the sacrificer becomes one with God. It is the giving itself of the lower to be a part of the higher, the yielding of the body as an instrument of the separated will to be an instrument of the divine Will, the presenting of men's " bodies as a living sacrifice, holy, acceptable unto God." [1] Thus it has been truly taught in the Church that those who rightly take part in the Eucharist enjoy a partaking of the Christ-life poured out for men. The transmuting of the lower into the higher is the object of this, as of all sacraments. The changing of the lower force by its union with the loftier is what is sought by those who participate

[1] Rom., xii, 1.
17

in it; and those who know the inner truth, and
realize the fact of the higher life, may in any religion,
by means of its sacraments, come into fuller, completer
touch with the divine Life that upholds the worlds, if
they bring to the rite the receptive nature, the act of
faith, the opened heart, which are necessary for the
possibilities of the sacrament to be realized.

The sacrament of marriage shows out the marks of a
sacrament as clearly and as definitely as do baptism and
the Eucharist. Both the outer sign and the inward
grace are there. The material is the ring—the circle
which is the symbol of the everlasting. The word of
power is the ancient formula. " In the Name of the
Father and of the Son, and of the Holy Ghost." The
sign of power is the joining of hands, symbolizing the
joining of the lives. These make up the outer essentials
of the sacrament.

The inner grace is the union of mind with mind, of
heart with heart, which makes possible the realization
of the unity of spirit, without which marriage is no
marriage, but a mere temporary conjunction of bodies.
The giving and receiving of the ring, the pronouncing
of the formula, the joining of hands, these form the
pictorial allegory; if the inner grace be not received, if
the participants do not open themselves to it by their
wish for the union of their whole natures, the sacrament
for them loses its beneficent properties, and becomes a
mere form.

But marriage has a yet deeper meaning; religions
with one voice have proclaimed it to be the image on

earth of the union between the earthly and the heavenly, the union between God and man. And even then its significance is not exhausted, for it is the image of the relation between Spirit and Matter, between the Trinity and the Universe. So deep, so far-reaching, is the meaning of the joining of man and woman in marriage.

Herein the man stands as representing the Spirit, the Trinity of Life, and the woman as representing the Matter, the Trinity of formative material. One gives life, the other receives and nourishes it. They are complementary to each other, two inseparable halves of one whole, neither existing apart from the other. As Spirit implies Matter and Matter Spirit, so husband implies wife and wife husband. As the abstract Existence manifests in two aspects, as a duality of Spirit and Matter, neither independent of the other, but each coming into manifestation with the other, so is humanity manifested in two aspects—husband and wife, neither able to exist apart, and appearing together. They are not twain but one, a dual-faced unity. God and the Universe are imaged in marriage; thus closely linked are husband and wife.

It is said above that marriage is also an image of the union between God and man, between the universal and the individualized Spirits. This symbolism is used in all the great scriptures of the world—Hindu, Hebrew, Christian. And it has been extended by taking the individualized Spirit as a Nation or a Church, a collection of such Spirits knit into a unity. So Isaiah declared to Israel: " Thy Maker is thine Husband; the Lord of hosts is His name. . . . As the bridegroom rejoiceth over the bride, so shall thy God rejoice over thee." [1]   So St. Paul wrote that the mystery of marriage represented Christ and the Church.[2]

If we think of Spirit and Matter as latent, unmanifested, then we see no production; manifested together, there is evolution.   And so when the halves of humanity are not manifested as husband and wife, there is no production of fresh life.   Moreover, they should be united in order that there may be a growth of life in each, a swifter evolution, a more rapid progress, by the half that each can give to each, each supplying what the other lacks.   The twain should be blended into one, setting forth the spiritual possibilities of man.   And they show forth also the perfect man, in whose nature Spirit and Matter are both completely developed and perfectly balanced, the divine man who unites in his own person husband and wife, the male and female elements in nature, as " God and Man are one Christ." [3]

---

[1] Isaiah, liv, 5; lxii, 5.

[2] Eph., v, 23-32.

[3] Athanasian Creed.

CHAPTER XIV

REVELATION

ALL the religions known to us are the custodians of sacred books, and appeal to these books for the settlement of disputed questions. They always contain the teachings given by the Founder of the religion, or by later teachers regarded as possessing superhuman knowledge. Even when a religion gives birth to many discordant sects, each sect will cling to the sacred canon, and will put upon its word the interpretation which best fits in with its own peculiar doctrines. However widely may be separated in belief the extreme Roman Catholic and the extreme Protestant, they both appeal to the same Bible. However far apart may be the philosophic Vedantin and the most illiterate Vallabhacharya, they both regard the same Vedas as supreme. However bitterly opposed to each other may be the Shias and the Sunnis, they both regard as sacred the same Koran. Controversies and quarrels may arise as to the meaning of texts, but the Book itself, in every case, is looked on with the utmost reverence. And rightly so; for all such books contain fragments of The Revelation, selected by One of the Great Ones who hold it in trust; such a fragment is embodied in what down here we call a Revelation, or a Scripture, and some part of the world rejoices in it as in a treasure of vast value. The fragment is chosen according to the needs of the time, the capacity of the people to whom it is given, the type of the race whom it is intended to instruct. It is generally given in a peculiar form, in which the outer history, or story, or song, or psalm, or prophecy, appears to the superficial or ignorant reader to be the whole book; but in these deeper meanings lie concealed, sometimes in numbers, sometimes in words constructed on a hidden plan —a cypher, in fact—sometimes in symbols, recognizable by the instructed, sometimes in allegories written as histories, and in many other ways. These books, indeed, have something of a sacramental character about them, an outer form and an inner life, an outer symbol and an inner truth. Those only can explain the hidden meaning who have been trained by those instructed in it; hence the dictum of St. Peter that " no prophecy of the Scripture is of any private interpretation." [1] The elaborate explanations of texts of the Bible, with which the volumes of patristic literature abound, seem fanciful and overstrained to the prosaic modern mind. The play upon numbers, upon letters, the apparently fantastic interpretations of paragraphs that, on the face of them, are ordinary historical statements of a simple character, exasperate the modern reader, who demands to have his facts presented clearly and coherently, and above all, requires what he feels to be solid ground under his feet. He declines absolutely to follow the light-footed mystic over what seem to him to be quaking

[1] II Pet., i, 20.

morasses, in a wild chase after dancing will-o'-the-wisps, which appear and disappear with bewildering and irrational caprice. Yet the men who wrote these exasperating treatises were men of brilliant intellect and calm judgment, the master-builders of the Church. And to those who read them aright they are still full of hints and suggestions, and indicate many an obscure pathway that leads to the goal of knowledge, and that might otherwise be missed.

We have already seen that Origen, one of the sanest of men, and versed in occult knowledge, teaches that the Scriptures are threefold, consisting of Body, Soul and Spirit.[1] He says that the Body of the Scriptures is made up of the outer words of the histories and the stories, and he does not hesitate to say that these are not literally true, but are only stories for the instruction of the ignorant. He even goes so far as to remark that statements are made in those stories that are obviously untrue, in order that the glaring contradictions that lie on the surface may stir people up to inquire as to the real meaning of these impossible relations. He says that so long as men are ignorant, the body is enough for them; it conveys teachings, it gives instructions, and they do not see the self-contradictions and impossibilities involved in the literal statements, and therefore are not disturbed by them. As the mind grows, as the intellect develops, these contradictions and impossibilities strike the attention, and bewilder the student; then he is stirred up to seek for a deeper meaning, and he

[1] See *Ante*, p. 70.

begins to find the soul of the Scriptures. That soul is the reward of the intelligent seeker, and he escapes from the bonds of the letter that killeth.[1] The spirit of the Scriptures may only be seen by the spiritually enlightened man; only those in whom the Spirit is evolved can understand the spiritual meaning: " The things of God knoweth no man but the Spirit of God . . . which things also we speak, not in the words which man's wisdom teacheth, but which the Holy Ghost teacheth." [2]

The reason for this method of revelation is not far to seek; it is the only way in which one teaching can be made available for minds at different stages of evolution, and thus train not only those to whom it is immediately given, but also those who, later in time, shall have progressed beyond those to whom the revelation was first made. Man is progressive; the outer meaning given long ago to unevolved men must needs be very limited, and unless something deeper and fuller than this outer meaning were hidden within it, the value of the Scripture would perish when a few millennia had passed away. Whereas by this method of successive meanings it is given a perennial value, and evolved men may find in it hidden treasures, until the day when, possessing the whole, they no longer need the part.

The world-Bibles, then, are fragments—fragments of revelation, and therefore are rightly described as revelation.

The next deeper sense of the word describes the mass of teaching held by the great Brotherhood of spiritual

---

[1] II Cor., iii, 6.   [2] I Cor., ii, 11, 13.

Teachers in trust for men; this teaching is embodied in books, written in symbols and in these is contained an account of kosmic laws, of the principles on which the kosmos is founded, of the methods by which it is evolved, of all the beings that compose it, of its past, its present, its future; this is The Revelation. This is the priceless treasure which the Guardians of humanity hold in charge, and from which they select, from time to time, fragments to form the Bibles of the world.

Third, the revelation, highest, fullest, best, is the Self-unveiling of Deity in the kosmos, the revealing of attribute after attribute, power after power, beauty after beauty, in all the various forms which in their totality compose the universe. He shows His splendour in the sun, His infinity in the star-flecked fields of space, His strength in mountains, His purity in snow-clad peaks and translucent air, His energy in rolling ocean-billows, His beauty in tumbling mountain torrent, in smooth, clear lake, in cool, deep forest and in sunlit plain, His fearlessness in the hero, His patience in the saint, His tenderness in mother-love, His protecting care in father and in king, His wisdom in the philosopher, His knowledge in the scientist, His healing power in the physician, His justice in the judge, His wealth in the merchant, His teaching power in the priest, His industry in the artisan. He whispers to us in the breeze, He smiles on us in the sunshine, He chides us in disease, He stimulates us, now by success, and now by failure. Everywhere and in everything He gives us glimpses of Himself to lure us on to love Him, and He hides Himself that we may learn to stand alone. To know Him everywhere is the true wisdom; to love Him everywhere is the true desire; to serve Him everywhere is the true action. This Self-revealing of God is the highest Revelation; all others are subsidiary and partial.

The inspired man is the man to whom some of this Revelation has come by the direct action of the universal Spirit on the separated Spirit that is His offspring, who has felt the illuminating influence of Spirit on Spirit. No man knows the truth so that he can never lose it, no man knows the truth so that he can never doubt it, until the revelation has come to him as though he stood alone on earth, until the Divine without has spoken to the Divine within, in the temple of the human heart, and the man thus knows by himself and not by another.

In a lesser degree a man is inspired when one greater than he stimulates within him powers which as yet are normally inactive, or even takes possession of him, temporarily using his body as a vehicle. Such an illuminated man, at the time of his inspiration, can speak that which is beyond his knowledge, and utter truths till then unguessed. Truths are sometimes thus poured out through a human channel for the helping of the world, and some One greater than the speaker sends down his life into the human vehicle, and they rush forth from human lips; then a great teacher speaks yet more greatly than he knows, the Angel of the Lord having touched his lips with fire.[1]   Such are the prophets of the race, who at some periods have spoken with overwhelming

[1] Isa., vi, 6, 7.

conviction, with clear insight, with complete understanding of the spiritual needs of man. Then the words live with a life immortal, and the speaker is truly a messenger from God. The man who has thus known can never again quite lose the memory of the knowledge, and he carries within his heart a certainty which can never quite disappear. The light may vanish and the darkness come down upon him; the gleam from heaven may fade and clouds may surround him; threat, question, challenge, may assail him; but within his heart there nestles the secret of peace—he knows, or knows that he has known.

That remembrance of true inspiration, that reality of the hidden life, has been put into beautiful and true words by Fredrick Myers, in his well-known poem, *St. Paul.* The apostle is speaking of his own experience, and is trying to give articulate expression to that which he remembers; he is figured as unable to thoroughly reproduce his knowledge, although he knows and his certainty does not waver:

> So, even I, athirst for His inspiring,
>   I, who have talked with Him, forget again;
> Yes, many days with sobs and with desiring,
>   Offer to God a patience and a pain.
>
> Then through the mid complaint of my confession,
>   Then through the pang and passion of my prayer,
> Leaps with a start the shock of His possession,
>   Thrills me and touches, and the Lord is there.
>
> Lo, if some pen should write upon your rafter
>   Mene and Mene in the folds of flame,
> Think ye could any memories thereafter
>   Wholly retrace the couplet as it came?

Lo, if some strange intelligible thunder
    Sang to the earth the secret of a star,
Scarce should ye catch, for terror and for wonder,
    Shreds of the story that was pealed so far!

Scarcely I catch the words of His revealing,
    Hardly I hear Him, dimly understand.
Only the power that is within me pealing
    Lives on my lips, and beckons to my hand.

Whoso hath felt the Spirit of the Highest
    Cannot confound, nor doubt Him, nor deny;
Yea, with one voice, O world, though thou deniest,
    Stand thou on that side, for on this am I.

Rather the world shall doubt when her retrieving
    Pours in the rain and rushes from the sod;
Rather than he in whom the great conceiving
    Stirs in his soul to quicken into God.

Nay, though thou then shouldst strike him from his glory,
    Blind and tormented, maddened and alone,
E'en on the cross would he maintain his story,
    Yes, and in Hell would whisper, " I have known."

Those who have in any sense realized that God is
around them, in them, and in everything, will be able
to understand how a place or an object may become
" sacred " by a slight objectivization of this perennial
universal Presence, so that those become able to sense
Him who do not normally feel His omnipresence. This
is generally effected by some highly advanced man, in
whom the inner Divinity is largely unfolded, and whose
subtle bodies are therefore responsive to the subtler
vibrations of consciousness. Through such a man, or
by such a man, spiritual energies may be poured forth,
and these will unite themselves with his pure vital
magnetism. He can then pour them forth on any object, and its ether and bodies of subtler matter will

become attuned to his vibrations, as before explained, and further, the Divinity within it can more easily manifest. Such an object becomes "magnetized", and, if this be strongly done, the object will itself become a magnetic centre, capable in turn of magnetizing those who approach it. Thus a body electrified by an electric machine will affect other bodies near which it may be placed.

An object thus rendered "sacred" is a very useful adjunct to prayer and meditation. The subtle bodies of the worshipper are attuned to its high vibrations, and he finds himself quieted, soothed, pacified, without effort on his own part. He is thrown into a condition in which prayer and meditation are easy and fruitful instead of difficult and barren, and an irksome exercise becomes insensibly delightful. If the object be a representation of some sacred Person—a crucifix, a Madonna and Child, an angel, a saint—there is a yet further gain. The being represented, if his magnetism has been thrown into the image by the appropriate word and sign of power, can reinforce that magnetism with a very slight expenditure of spiritual energy, and may thus influence the devotee, or even show himself through the image, when otherwise he would not have done so. For in the spiritual world economy of forces is observed, and a small amount of energy will be expended where a larger would be withheld.

An application of these same occult laws may be made to explain the use of all consecrated objects—relics, amulets, etc. They are all magnetized objects, more or less powerful, or useless, according to the knowledge, purity, and spirituality of the person who magnetizes them.

Places may similarly be made sacred, by the living in them of saints, whose pure magnetism, radiating from them, attunes the whole atmosphere to peace-giving vibrations. Sometimes holy men, or beings from the higher worlds, will directly magnetize a certain place, as in the case mentioned in the Fourth Gospel, where an angel came at a certain season and touched the water, giving it healing qualities.[1] In such places even careless worldly men will sometimes feel the blessed influence, and will be temporarily softened and inclined towards higher things. The divine Life in each man is ever trying to subdue the form, and mould it into an expression of itself; and it is easy to see how that Life will be aided by the form being thrown into vibrations sympathetic with those of a more highly evolved being, its own efforts being reinforced by a stronger power. The outer recognition of this effect is a sense of quiet, calm, and peace; the mind loses its restlessness, the heart its anxiety. Anyone who observes himself will find that some places are more conducive to calm, to meditation, to religious thought, to worship, than others. In a room, a building, where there has been a great deal of worldly thought, of frivolous conversation, of mere rush of ordinary worldly life, it is far harder to quiet the mind and to concentrate the thought, than in a place where religious thought has been carried on year after

[1] St. John, v, 4.

year, century after century; there the mind becomes calm and tranquil, and that which would have demanded serious effort in the first place is done without effort in the second.

This is the rationale of places of pilgrimage, of temporary retreats into seclusion; the man turns inward to seek the God within him, and is aided by the atmosphere created by thousands of others who before him have sought the same in the same place. For in such a place there is not only the magnetization produced by a single saint, or by the visit of some great being of the invisible world; each person, who visits the spot with a heart full of reverence and devotion, and is attuned to his vibrations, reinforces those vibrations with his own life, and leaves the spot better than it was when he came to it. Magnetic energy slowly disperses, and a sacred object or place becomes gradually demagnetized if put aside or deserted. It becomes more magnetized as it is used or frequented. But the presence of the ignorant scoffer injures such objects and places, by setting up antagonistic vibrations which weaken those already existing there. As a wave of sound may be met by another which extinguishes it, and the result is silence, so do the vibrations of the scoffing thought weaken or extinguish the vibrations of the reverent and loving one. The effect produced will, of course, vary with the relative strengths of the vibrations, but the mischievous one cannot be without result, for the laws of vibration are the same in the higher worlds as in the physical, and thought vibrations are the expression of real energies.

The reason and the effect of the consecration of churches, chapels, cemeteries, will now be apparent. The act of consecration is not the mere public setting aside of a place for a particular purpose; it is the magnetization of the place for the benefit of all those who frequent it. For the visible and the invisible worlds are interrelated, interwoven, each with each, and those can best serve the visible by whom the energies of the invisible can be wielded.

AFTERWORD

WE have reached the end of a small book on a great
subject, and have only lifted a corner of the veil that
hides the Virgin of Eternal Truth from the careless eyes
of men. The hem of her garment only has been seen,
heavy with gold, richly dight with pearls. Yet even this,
as it waves slowly, breathes out celestial fragrances—
the sandal and rose-attar of fairer worlds than ours.
What should be the unimaginable glory, if the veil were
lifted, and we saw the splendour of the Face of the
Divine Mother, and in Her arms the Child who is the
very Truth? Before that Child the Seraphim ever veil
their faces; who then of mortal birth may look on Him
and live?

Yet since in man abides His very Self, who shall forbid him to pass within the veil, and to see with " open
face the glory of the Lord "? From the Cave to highest
Heaven; such was the pathway of the Word made Flesh,
and known as the Way of the Cross. Those who share
the manhood share also the Divinity, and may tread
where He has trodden. " What Thou art, That am I."

PEACE TO ALL BEINGS.

INDEX

INDEX

A Quest for Christianity

CALL TO THE HEIGHTS
by Geoffrey Hodson
A teacher to pupil, step by step book of instructions on how to awaken our individual divine consciousness.

CHRIST LIFE FROM NATIVITY TO ASCENSION
by Geoffrey Hodson
An insightful consideration of the New Testament.

FIRE OF CREATION
by J. J. van der Leeuw
An examination of the universe as a dynamic process based upon spiritual principles, and emphasizing the Holy Ghost as a possible feminine principle of nature.

HIDDEN WISDOM IN THE HOLY BIBLE,
VOLUMES I, II, III and IV
by Geoffrey Hodson
An esoteric study of Biblical allegory, the alternative to a literal interpretation.

INSIGHTS FOR THE AGE OF AQUARIUS
by Gina Cerminara
How the science of General Semantics reveals and corrects many ambiguities in the Holy Bible.

Available from
QUEST BOOKS
306 W. Geneva Rd.
Wheaton, IL 60187